PSYCHOANALYTIC TECHNIQUE WITH CHILDREN, ADOLESCENTS, AND ADULTS:

AN INTRODUCTION FOR STUDENTS AND PROFESSIONALS

IVAN SHERICK, Ph.D.

PSYCHOANALYTIC TECHNIQUE WITH CHILDREN, ADOLESCENTS, AND ADULTS:

AN INTRODUCTION FOR STUDENTS AND PROFESSIONALS

IVAN SHERICK, Ph.D.

IPBOOKS.net
International Psychoanalytic Books

International Psychoanalytic Books
IPBooks.net
30-27 33rd Street
Astoria, NY 11102

Publisher:
  International Psychoanalytic Books (IPBooks)
  30-27 33rd Street, Astoria, NY 11102.
  Online at: http://www.IPBooks.net

ISBN: 978-0-9995965-5-5

Table Of Contents

Preface   1

Part One
Psychoanalytic Concepts of Development   5
Psychoanalytic Model of the Mind   9

Part Two
Referral   15
Evaluation   17
Recommendation   21
The Frame   23
The Beginning of an Analysis   27
Establishing Working Alliance   31
Resistance   34
Transference   40
Real Object, Developmental Object, &
     Transference Object   44
Countertransference   46
Interpretation   49
Acting Out   58
Limit Setting   60
Ways of Bringing Material   66
Comings & Goings   73
Role of Education   75
Work with Parents   78
Goals of Psychoanalytic Treatment   82
Working Through   85
Termination   87

Part Three
    Brief Clinical Illustrations   93

Part Four
    Other Schools of Psychoanalysis   111

Part Five
    The Widening Spectrum of Psychoanalytic
        Treatment   117

Part Six
    Dealing with Illness & Death   121
    A Professional Will   123
    Planned Retirement of the Analyst   124
    Negative Therapeutic Reaction   125
    "Soul Murder"   126
    Diversity   127

Part Seven
    Postscript   131

Representative List of Topics   135
Recommended Readings   141

Preface

I have decided to write this Introduction following the positive reception of a recent earlier book, *Introduction to Child, Adolescent, and Adult Development: A Psychoanalytic Perspective for Students and Professionals*, published by IP Books. That book was written in a "reader-friendly" manner. I used technical language with clear and simple definitions, did not include references, or footnotes, and it was not styled as an academic scholarly treatise. I have endeavored to write this book in the same fashion. Technical terms are italicized.

I have not divided the book up into respective child, adolescent, and adult sections. My thinking is that by not doing so, the differences and similarities in child, adolescent and adult psychoanalysis with regard to a specific technique will be more available to the reader if they are addressed together. In my opinion awareness of child and adolescent analysis is beneficial, and I would say essential, to effective work with adults. The reason is that when one treats an adult one is dealing predominantly with the child and/or the adolescent within the adult.

My focus is on psychoanalysis as a clinical technique, so I will not get involved in a discussion of psychoanalytically informed clinical treatments, e.g., psychodynamic psychotherapy. There are some similarities but also major differences. I will have an introductory section on the psychoanalytic model of the mind and developmental theory. I think this will help the reader appreciate the discussion of the various techniques because it will provide a theoretical framework or rationale of the reasons for the various interventions. The topics I have chosen to focus on are inspired by my experience completing a Hampstead Index as a requirement of my child/adolescent analytic training program.

You will notice that some issues are mentioned several times in different contexts. This is so because they have relevance for different types of analytic interventions. Psychoanalytic clinical theory and technical interventions recognize the multi-determined nature of mental conflict and its treatment and some issues reappear because they are part of this multi-determinism.

At the end of the book I will include a list of references of books on psychoanalytic technique that I have felt helpful in my career as a psychoanalyst.

I received my training first as a Child & Adolescent Analyst at The Hampstead Clinic in London, England, under Miss Anna Freud's direction, graduating in 1971. I then received my Adult Psychoanalytic training from the Michigan Psychoanalytic Institute, graduating in 1981. My psychoanalytic orientation is known as an *ego-psychological* one, derived from the *classical* technique formulated by Sigmund Freud, but I believe it is better described as a *contemporary ego-psychological* orientation insofar as I have integrated some perspectives of techniques of other contemporary schools of psychoanalysis. I will briefly mention other schools of psychoanalysis so the reader can choose to read up more on them if my brief comments raise his or her curiosity.

I am grateful to past supervisors, colleagues and patients whom I have learned from over the past years. I hope this book will be helpful to you in decisions you face regarding professional training or personal growth.

Part One

Psychoanalytic Concepts of Development

I offer this brief account of psychoanalytic concepts because later in my exposition of psychoanalytic technique you will understand, I hope, that technique and the theoretical concepts of the mind go together like "hand in glove," to use a metaphor. Our techniques have grown out of our experience in observing how patients have reacted, i.e., how their minds have reacted, to our interventions. Such observations have resulted in modifications to our theory of the mind, and to developing modifications in technique.

I will give a synopsis of the psychoanalytic theory of development, emphasizing child and adolescent development. When I discuss the aims of child and adolescent psychoanalytic technique you will have this as a context to understand the rationale underlying the interventions more fully.

As a child physically matures there is a sequence of bodily *erogenous zones* that the child experiences. Psychoanalysts call this sequence *psychosexual phases of development.* The drive involved is the sexual one; in psychoanalytic theory it is called the *libidinal drive.* The body and the mind are synergistic, i.e., the effects of the two are integrated. At first, the mouth area is the locus of oral sensations that are erogenous and the height of these sensations are between birth and two years. This *oral phase* corresponds with nursing at the breast or bottle. Next is the *anal phase* (2-3 years of age) and the anus is the focus of intense erogenous sensations and corresponds roughly with a child undergoing toilet mastery. The next phase (3-5 years of age) is a focus on the genitals and urination for each gender. This phase was called the *phallic phase* when it was erroneously believed that both genders highly valued the male genital. This has been revised as we learn that both genders value their respective genitals. Children can be observed to touch this area of their bodies. The Oedipal phase follows (roughly between three and 5 years of age) and has to do with competitive feelings with the parent of the same gender for the prerogatives of physical intimacy that the parent of the same gender as the child has with the other parent. There are wishes to make or receive a baby with the parent of the opposite gender, and feelings of threat from the parent of the same gender because this desire is considered forbidden. Sometimes the phases overlap a bit and life events such as early or delayed maturational changes and unpredictable external events may disrupt the continuous nature of development throughout the life span and be transformative. A transformation could be positive (e.g., the remission of a serious illness) or negative (e.g., identification with the aggressor). So while continuity is fundamental, it is not all-inclusive.

While the libidinal drive and its derivatives are thought to motivate much behavior, the aggressive drive and its derivatives are believed to be paramount in human motivation too. It is these two drives that psychoanalytic clinical investigation has clarified to be the major movers of human behavior.

Drives have a *source* that is the bodily zone it originates from, an *aim*, which is to seek gratification, an *economic* or quantitative intensity, and an *object* or the venue for achieving satisfaction or gratification. Implicit is a demand on the Ego to obtain gratification for the drive.

Two important life events are *fixation* to a phase and *regression* to fixation points. Later when I discuss the aims of child analysis you will understand how the techniques are strategies to help children reduce the effects of fixation and regression. We know from extensive generations of analytic work with adults about the validity of the above developmental concepts. Not to have experienced the Oedipal Complex is a disadvantage for a child, as can sometimes result in situations when parents are divorced. A consequence of the partial dissolution of the Oedipal consequence is the *internalization* of sanctions against incestuous desires, which is the beginning of the conscience (Superego). A conscience is imperative for the regulation and control of drives.

A *fixation* occurs when during a particular psychosexual phase a child experiences either too much or too little gratification from the external world with regard to drives stemming from the phase that the child is then in. A fixation on a particular phase is a "readiness" that reactivates itself, so that derivatives from that psychosexual phase strive for gratification, when a person feeling stress regresses to a fixation point. We know that there is a reverse relationship between the amount of deprivation or gratification of drive derivatives of a particular psychosexual phase and the emergence of a fixation based on the constitutional strength of the particular psychosexual phase. For example, we know that some children are born with a strong anal drive and it takes little control management by their parent during toilet mastery to result in the child's frustration and to result in developing a fixation. On the contrary, for those children with a weak anal constitution lots of control by the parent will not affect the child. We call this reverse etiological relationship the *complemental series*. A child analyst hearing examples of toilet mastery attempts by a parent, can identify a child with a strong anal constitution and advise the parent to "go slow," letting the child set their own pace in controlling his or her bowels.

Latency corresponds with beginning of elementary school and during years six to puberty the erotic desires go "under ground" (*repressed*). The relative strengths of the Ego vs. the Id are reversed in favor of the Ego during these years. Hence, the ego is less burdened with controlling libidinal drive expression. The child is learning about the external world and strengthening the repository of defenses to prepare for puberty and the regaining of ascendency of the strength of the *drives* over the executive part of the mind, the Ego.

Puberty roughly starts adolescence. During the years from puberty to around twenty years of age, the mind is dealing with mastering important issues like masturbation, sexual orientation, choosing a partner not based on a former relationship with a parent, i.e., choosing a non-incestuous relationship, becoming independent, more-or-less from parents, recognizing and accepting that one is not omnipotent and not needing to resort to self-aggrandizing fantasies and behavior, strengthening cognitive abilities so that abstract thinking is available on a reliable basis, etc. Again, psychoanalytic interventions are aimed at helping an adolescent accomplish these developmental achievements.

Adults also go through developmental stages that are psycho-socially driven, as well as due to the waning of a youthful body. Thus, parenthood, choice of an occupation, dealing with an "empty nest", retirement, deaths of parents, grand parenting, and coming to terms with death, are some of the issues adults deal with developmentally. Again, psychoanalysis helps adults deal with such issues along with helping them to achieve more adaptive solutions to neurotic conflict.

Psychoanalytic Model of the Mind

Our model of the mind is that it consists primarily of an unconscious part, the *Unconscious* (Ucs), a *Preconscious* part (Pcs), and a *Conscious* part (Cs). A metaphor would be an iceberg, i.e., with the major part of an iceberg being underwater and not seen, which corresponds to the Ucs. The remainder of the mind like the iceberg is partially underwater, capable of being above water, the Pcs., or always above water, the Cs. This formulation of the mind is known as a *topographic* model. Nowadays, we think of *psychic structures*, the *Id*, corresponding to the unconscious part of the mind, and to the *Superego* and *Ego*, both predominantly conscious parts of the mind. Now we refer to them as "structures" to connote that they are mental entities enduring over time, known as a *structural* model of the mind. Most contemporary analysts prefer the structural model but some, like myself, are comfortable using both.

The Id is that part of the mind where instinctual wishes reside, from birth and evolving over the lifetime as the individual matures. These wishes are capable of being accepted into consciousness under certain circumstances, although some of earliest origin, before a child has words, may never reach the conscious part of the mind, although derivatives may. Also residing are wishes that have been expelled from conscious part of the mind because of certain circumstances. Drives make demands upon the Ego to be put into action and to be gratified. The way drives are gratified is for *objects* to be sought to gratify them. People are referred to as objects to distinguish them from the subject.

The Superego is the structure of the mind that essentially is the *conscience.* Early on its moral imperatives are unrealistic and primitive, like "an eye for an eye," but as the individual matures they do as well, becoming more relative, less absolute. An individual with a mature Superego is capable of forgiving himself or herself after he or she recognize they have felt remorse and made amends for transgressions. Once forgiving oneself, it is easier to forgive others. When a Superego "rule" is not adhered to an individual feels *guilt.* A related feeling is *shame.* It seems to have an earlier origin developmentally than guilt. The feeling of shame is that it is believed to be visible to onlookers whereas guilt is more private. The *Ego Ideal* is based on internalized images of "heroes" we wish to be like.

The Ego is the executive part of the mind. It is where so-called executive functions are carried out. The functions we refer to are reality testing, judgment, rational thinking, problem solving, perception, audition, speech, motility, and concerns about perceived safety with the employment of ego defenses to insure it.

Reality testing underscores how the Ego becomes aware of both the external and internal worlds. A child is impacted by events in the external world much more than an adult. Children are more dependent on the external world to gratify their needs. The external and internal worlds can introduce different demands on the Ego, a recipe for *conflict.* The *synthetic function* of the ego brings together these different demands and conflict takes place. What follows is the defensive functioning of the Ego.

The Ego gives meaning to exchanges between the internal and external worlds when drives demand it execute actions to satisfy the drives via objects. These meanings are experienced as *feelings* or *affects.* A theory of affects has not been thoroughly exposited; some object to defining affects as derivatives of the drives. I believe they are intimately connected via the dynamics of drive arousal. There are primarily two types of thinking, *primary process* and *secondary process.* The former is operative in the unconscious part of the mind, the Id, and the latter primarily in the Ego. In primary process thinking things like cause and effect are abandoned, a single event can stand for all events, what happed in the past is treated as if it happened presently, etc. This kind of thinking often enters into *fantasy*, also in *dreams*, and in a *parapraxsis* (so called "slips of the tongue"). Secondary thinking includes logic, cause and effect, deductive and inductive reasoning, abstract thinking, symbolic thinking, considerations of time and space, etc. In other words, primary process thinking is "primitive" and secondary process thinking is "mature" or advanced. We also conceptualize the *Self*, a sense of one's own *identity*, a *self-image*, and the site of self-esteem, empowerment, and subjectivity. *Identifications* are an important aspect of self-identity. People modify their self-image to take in aspects of people they love, revere, frightened by, whom they have "lost" from separation, etc.

A related mental structure to the *Ego Ideal* is the *Ideal Self*. This refers to what self image an individual aspires to but seldom reaches. It is the image of narcissistic perfection. If the discrepancy is too great between the actual self and the ideal self, an individual can become despondent. *Narcissism* is a positive feeling about the self. We posit that the pleasure an infant feels when gratified, before a clear distinction between oneself and the external world, is attributed to oneself. We call this *primary narcissism*. Presumably there exists a sense of *omnipotence*. Once the external world is distinguished and gratification comes from an external source and pleasure is experienced this is *secondary narcissism*. It can be depleted if the parents become less responsive to the child's needs. We conjecture that omnipotence is attributed to the parents that reduce drive demands. Later, acceptance by the Superego enhances secondary narcissism. Human beings mature and develop, as they get older. The infant gradually develops a mature ego, but early on the caregiver, usually the mother, serves as an auxiliary ego. This is essential insofar as the child has not yet sufficiently developed and consolidated a defensive repertoire to deal with both the internal and external world. The human mind operates under a *pleasure principle* so that the ego does not tolerate "unpleasure," such as anxiety, guilt, shame, etc. Mental conflict ensues when there is a wish that a person senses is contrary to the rules of the external world or the internal world, the conscience. I say "senses" because often a conscious thought process does not occur. There occurs a feeling of anxiety followed by a sense of imminent danger, either real or imagined. If the wish is expressed in action, the sense is that punishment will follow, either abandonment, loss of love, physical bodily punishment, or feelings of guilt. Mental conflict is experienced. Hence the wish must be modified, a compromise is accepted, often a neurotic one. A neurotic symptom is such a compromise, consisting of a derivative of the prohibited wish, modified by the defensive maneuver of the Ego. The compromise formation is capable of evoking some partial gratification and attendant pleasure. Much of psychoanalytic technique, you will see, has to do with helping analysands, regardless of their age, to understand their mind and how it deals with mental conflict, the compromise solutions they have come up with, and a recognition that their automatic neurotic solutions are not in their best interest. With analytic processing of their mental life they come to accept that they will become capable of recognizing neurotic solutions in more rapid time, and choose better solutions. With younger children they recognize that they can express themselves in ways that more likely will end with their wishes being satisfied and insuring feelings of safety. Young children can appreciate that their Superego, their "inner policeman," need not be so harsh. In psychoanalytic treatment we hope that patients of all ages will be more tolerant of desires, the content of the Id, tolerate frustration better, that they will come to understand that they need to recognize a difference between a deed and a thought, and that a mature conscience, the Superego, operates mainly on relative standards and not absolute standards of right and wrong. They learn to "tolerate" anxiety more and to modify *instinctual* aims so that they are less immature and selfish and more socially acceptable (*sublimation*). In psychoanalysis we have a belief in *psychic determinism*, a concept that all mental life and behavior has a meaning, is determined by a psychological cause that may or may not be understood. (This is not to deny the causative properties of an individual's biology.)

Part Two

Referral

When an adult telephones it is a simple matter of finding a mutually convenient time to meet to learn what is being sought. Occasionally, there will be an inquiry about what your fee is and if you are on a particular insurance panel. If not, it might mean the end of the contact, unless you are prepared to offer that you would consider a reduced fee. Many prospective patients will accept that and schedule an introductory session.

With children it is more complicated. Of course, a young child, or for that matter, even an adolescent, does not contact a psycho-analyst independently. A parent usually establishes the initial contact. Sometimes, it may be a single parent but often it may be one spouse of a married couple. It is essential in cases of divorced parents to learn if both parents are in favor of an evaluation. I indicate that I will need to see or hear from the divorced spouse to get confirmation that both parents are in favor of an evaluation. Sometimes one parent has been given legal responsibility for medical decisions regarding the child. A professional asked to do an evaluation must ascertain this.

With children under the age of twelve I see the parent(s) first and then the child. With children older than this I most often elect to see the child first and later the parent(s). Children who are late latency or older are beginning to feel a need to become more independent from parents and I think it is helpful to convey support of this developmental need. Most parents understand this rationale and support it. In these cases I will answer any questions a parent might have about my fee and fee policies so they can decide whether or not to go ahead with the evaluation.

I try to schedule appointments at a time that is not disruptive of a child's or adolescent's school schedule so as not to introduce practical issues that would complicate the need to go ahead. Later, if treatment has started and the parents or child complain of competing interests after school that interfere with treatment appointments, I approach such complaints as *resistance* (more about this later).

Evaluation

In an evaluation a psychoanalyst wants to determine if psycho-analysis is the treatment of choice for the patient. We call this assessing the *analyzability* of patients. There are some diagnostic issues that some analysts consider contrary to a choice of analysis as the preferred treatment. In recent years the scope has widened of diagnostic categories deemed likely to benefit from psychoana-lytic intervention. Some traumas are felt to have had irreversible consequences and not remediable by analysis. Some would say that a *trial of analysis* is warranted for all patients. This belief assumes that it is wrong to use theory to predict outcomes. Empirical results should be the criteria. There are too many false negatives. Often, patient histories contain determinants that suggest a bad outcome. Nevertheless, there are some criteria that we can employ.

Sometimes after a first meeting the "fit" between analyst and prospective *analysand* (term refers to patients in analysis) seems workable and other times it may seem impossible or doubtful. By "fit" I mean something intangible; it is a sense that this is a person I can feel comfortable with to talk about myself an/or to listen to. Both the analyst and prospective analysand should evaluate the "fit." It makes sense to me to not come to a conclusion after one meeting.

Psychoanalysis, in my opinion, in best suited for *neurotic* diag-noses that suggest mental conflict. This is so because we hope the adult does not have serious cognitive disabilities resulting from a brain illness, serious impairment of intelligence, severe distortions of the perception of reality, criminal psychopathic pathology, severe autism, and other impairments that would make it difficult for the patient to endure the relative lack of gratification that is part of psychoanalytic technique. What I mean is that an analyst is guided by a *rule of abstinence*. What is meant is that the expectation is that the future analysand will be able to deal with the frustration resulting from the analyst's not granting requests for gratification of wishes, or providing answers to curiosity about the life of the analyst, the lack of advice given by the analyst, etc. The abstinence is a therapeutic strategy that aims to re-create in a manageable way the conditions perceived by the analysand to have caused "problems" in the first place. Conflict is re-experienced, neurotic compromises occur, resistance is experienced, transference develops, and so on.

There are analysts who have worked with psychotic patients, as well as severely delinquent adolescents, who claim positive results with modifications of technique. Psychoanalytically informed treatments, namely, psychodynamic psychotherapy, will be used with patients it is felt would not benefit from classical psychoanalysis but would from the above.

Some children, such as those who have been abused, traumatized, handicapped (e.g., by blindness), or deprived as youngsters of adults who could serve as *auxiliary egos* for them, will need a form of reparative therapy, that strengthens their Ego before child analysis can be the treatment of choice. In most instances, the history provided by the parents and prospective analysands themselves will allow you to rule out some prospective patients from the start.

With an adult, an analyst might begin by asking the person "How can I be of help to you?" Adults will then begin to tell a story of who they are, what troubles them and the changes being sought. As an analyst, one listens and on occasion asks a question to clarify something. An analyst does not have a checklist of questions and I discourage taking notes. One might ask a question if you have a diagnostic issue that you wish to clarify. For example, if adults volunteer that they are depressed and have suicidal thoughts, the analyst may wish to know if a suicide plan is in effect to ascertain the seriousness of the depression. If serious, a psychiatric referral may be called for.

It may be necessary to see a prospective adult analysand multiple times. The patient is informed about this at the end of the first session. I also inquire if the patient has felt comfortable talking to me. I indicate that during the consultative time the adult can evaluate if the feel that they can work with me, feel comfortable talking to me, and that I, too, will evaluate our "fit." I think this underscores the importance of the relationship between analysand and analyst.

With adolescents, there is a lot of similarity with the consultation stage with an adult. Many adolescents are very forthcoming about their unhappiness and offer their understanding as to the genesis of the unhappiness. At the end of the consultation, which may be after several sessions, and a recommendation for treatment is proposed, I mention that confidentiality will be respected. I indicate that there will be one exception, namely, if I felt that their safety was in jeopardy, e.g., because of a suicide plan, I would notify the parents of this situation. In my experience most adolescents accept this. I also indicate that I will be meeting with the adolescent's parents on a regular basis to help them with issues of parenting. I indicate if there has been a rupture in the relationship between the adolescent and parent(s), one aim will be to restore a growth promoting one. Again, most adolescents accept this. I would not say this if I believed that a parent(s) has had a toxic effect on their child and they are unlikely to change.

With a young child, in the consultation phase with parents, I listen to the reasons for seeking an evaluation. I try to assess the correspondence between the two parents. I listen to their personal histories as younger persons. They may not volunteer a personal history during the consultative phase, and may need to feel more comfortable with me to do so. Most parents will convey the parental interventions they have tried with their child to ameliorate the problems that they come to me for help.

With parents of a young child, I ask them what they have told their child as the reasons they are seeking professional help. With some parents I learn that nothing has been said, that they were waiting to talk to me first before telling their child they are seeking help. Exploring their ideas about options conveys a lot about their parenting styles. Also, it is important to focus on both strengths and weaknesses in parenting during these early evaluation sessions. Focusing only on weaknesses makes parents feel guilty and less hopeful.

It is important for the psychoanalyst of potential analysands of all ages to be tolerant with ambiguity and uncertainty. Likely, there will be some questions in the mind of the evaluating psychoanalyst about the genesis of the issues that the adults, adolescents, and children and their parents are seeking help about. But, patience is required because the mind in conflict requires it. I will speak to more about this later.

Recommendation

A psychoanalyst may come to the belief that the patient being evaluated would best be helped by a psychoanalytic intervention. The next step is to make this recommendation to the patient, and in the case of a young child, to the parent(s). With an adolescent I will tell them first, with an understanding that to proceed, we need the agreement of his or her parent(s).

Many parents will agree immediately, but others, understandably, may ask questions, such as, "Why four or five times weekly?" Here the analyst needs to convey in an intelligible way about the essence of a psychoanalytic immersion, how it works and the conditions under which it is most effective. I point out that their child (adolescent) is dealing with mental conflict.

I then define "mental conflict" as a conflict between competing wishes and demands in the mind causing unpleasant emotional feelings such as anxiety, guilt, shame, or embarrassment. I point out, e.g., there may be a wish to express anger or a sexual desire but a part of the mind surmises that if the thought was expressed in action the external world or internal world, e.g., the conscience, would object and the unpleasant feelings would intensify. I indicate that many of these wishes in the form of thoughts or fantasies may not be conscious but are unconscious. To deal with these mental conflicts, people come up with neurotic "solutions" that are not adaptive or in their best interests; they are compromise solutions satisfying both the wish and the opposing, often imagined, force. The aim of psychoanalysis is to help an individual to tolerate thought and fantasies and accept them as non-actions, and come up with more adaptive solutions. This seems to make sense to most adults and adolescents. It is not unusual for parents to believe that if their child were more obedient then there would be no "problems" for their child. For many parents it is comforting for them to hear that their child is having worries because of mental conflict, not because of "bad" parenting or because of disobedience.

When a recommendation for analysis is made many parents and adults will ask, "How long will it take?" I respond that is a good question, and then I tell them that it is like asking someone how long will it take to walk from point A to point B? The answer is that one can give the distance but the time to walk it depends on the length of stride of the walker. The duration, then, depends on how well one works in the analysis. For some adults it seems counter-intuitive to revisit the past during which they encountered unhappiness. When they are told, however, if the past is not emotionally understood it repeats itself in the present, this makes sense to them. During analysis, both analyst and analysand become aware that "slow and steady wins the race;" change takes time because the natural resistance needs to become less formidable so that the analysand "wants" to change.

With younger children, during the evaluation I ask them what their parent(s) told them was the reason for them seeing me. Some can discuss what they were told; others say they do not know. Then I ask them for their understanding about why they were sent to see me. Based on what they say, I try to engage them in a dialogue as to whether, e.g., getting angry or not paying attention, is the best way to deal with what got them upset? Perhaps, I suggest, there are different and better ways to take care of what made them upset? I might mention a fictitious child, Freddy, I know who when he got angry about something would say, "I'm angry." This would get the attention of the person he was angry towards or the attention of a parent or teacher and they would help Freddy so he got a turn to play with a toy that another child would not allow. I tell the child that I would like to help him or her to learn ways to deal with angry or sad feeling or other bad feelings. Most children accept this.

The Frame

When the recommendation for analysis is made with adults and accepted, at that point, the *frame* of the treatment is presented. The "frame" is sort of the contract or the parameters of the treatment that the prospective analysand agrees to, or request further discussion, hoping for a modification. The frame includes the appointment schedule, my fee policy, legal holidays that I do not work, and likely vacation times that I will be taking. With children, the frame is mainly discussed with the parent(s). I will convey the appointment schedule with a young child. With an adolescent, I will discuss the frame as well, acknowledging that their parents will have ultimate responsibility about my fee but they will be asked to bring in the check.

Issues of confidentiality are part of the frame. With adults it is pretty implicit but may have to be underscored with some who question the issue. Below, when I discuss parent work I will point out the limits on confidentiality. In my work with children and adolescents I regard the child or adolescent as the patient. Parent work, however, is essential in psychoanalytic work with children and adolescents. When explaining the limits on their confidentiality to parents, they may disclose what they divulged is a secret, a *family secret*. The analyst will appreciate that much more work with the parents will be necessary before the family secret can be told to the child. The parents will be encouraged to disclose it to their child and to answer questions. Presumably in most instances the child or adolescent will bring the "secret" into their treatment.

When a recommendation for analysis is made to prospective analysands and to parents, the question is often asked about the frequency of sessions. They want to know the rationale. Why are four or five sessions weekly required? How can a child come in so often when he or she is engaged in after-school activities? The concept of immersion then needs to be explained. Essentially the analyst talks about topics receding back into defended area of the mind, if there are long time intervals between sessions. If the interruption is brief then the scary topic is less likely to be hidden away and will be more accessible to the analysand and therefore more likely to be resumed as a communication to the analyst. Most adults can appreciate this, along with older adolescents. Younger children feel less safe in talking about scary topics and worry about intrusions on their free time after school. The analyst will need to point out to the child what has been learned during the consultation that has shed light onto the difficulties the child came in with and which immersion can provide him or her with help. Some children and adolescents still balk but many welcome being rid of their distress. The analyst also hopes that the parents of the hesitant child will come to their side and support the immersion. Sometimes it is best to postpone beginning with a child or adolescent until the parents have entered into a *working alliance* (more below) with the analyst.

The "frame" is important because after adults or parents accept it (with adolescents and children mainly the frequency of sessions) if not complied with this action has an important meaning in the ongoing analysis of them or their child. It is a form of "resistance," particularly in the form of *acting out* (more later) that needs to be addressed by the analyst insofar as it suggests uneasiness about being in analysis or having a child in analysis. If not addressed it can undermine and even disrupt the analysis.

One issue of the frame merits further discussion, mainly because of the variability of position on it by different psychoanalysts. This has to do with cancellations. I indicate that analysands, or parents, will be charged for all scheduled sessions, with out regard for the reason for the cancellation. I also make it known that I will not charge them if I use their appointment time to schedule another consultation. I also indicate I will make an attempt to reschedule them if they request it. Also, when I cancel they will not be charged. I have arrived at this policy over the years experimenting with other ones, e.g., no charge if given advance warning, such as twenty-four hours, of a cancellation. My thoughts are that there are reasonable causes for a cancellation, e.g., a sick child, a flat tire, the death of a relative, etc., but I do not think it is in the best interest of the analyst or the analysand to have to make a judgment call as to what is "reasonable or not." The parameter of fee policy is part of the business arrangement or contract between the analyst and the analysand and subjectivity should not be a part of it. Another aspect of the fee policy is time of payment. I present a bill at the last session of the month and request payment by the fifth calendar day of the next month. Again, there are other ways to handle this, e.g., payment expected on the last scheduled session of the month. Late payment, as discussed above, may be a form of resistance.

The analyst's office is also part of the frame. One does not meet with an adult at a coffee shop, with an adolescent at the Mall, with a child at the playground. The office is constant and is a "boundary" of sorts for the analysis. The analyst's office is devoid of very personal things like family photos or memorabilia, in order to not interfere with the fantasies of the analysand and his or her curiosity about the analyst. Soundproofing is secure so sounds from an adjacent office are not heard, and the analysand is confident what is said will not be heard from another office. Usually, a waiting room is provided with double doors between it and the consultation room. When analysts share office space there is sometimes a common waiting area that I think is not favorable because of issues of confidentiality. I think it is ideal to have a separate entrance door and exit door so analysands are less likely to bump into each other between sessions. Analysts that elect to have a home office, as I have, are aware that the analysand is more privy to the analyst's personal tastes than an office in an office building.

Child analysts best have an area separate from the area they see adults and adolescents in, because of the scattered toys that need to be cleaned up after a session or between sessions. Also, some children do not adhere to the limit that they can say anything but not do anything in the treatment area. Hence, an analyst who also sees adults and adolescents would not want to expose a child to his office where the child may break a valuable art object or scratch furniture, or tear a carpet, or put crayon marks on a wall in a fit of anger.

I do not take notes during sessions and do not encourage supervisees to do so either. I think it distracts from your attention to the analysand and I know I would not like it if I was the analysand. What is in the analyst's mind is what will be used in interventions. In between sessions, notes can be written that are considered important to refresh one's memory. Some analysts see patients back-to-back, but I prefer a five or ten minute interval.

The Beginning of an Analysis

Psychoanalysts differ as to what they convey to analysands when they begin psychoanalysis. Some choose to say nothing about the process or procedure and wait for the analysand to ask questions about how to begin. After all, the couch is within sight in the office and there have been scores of movies showing patients lying on their backs on an analytic couch with the analyst behind them out of their sight. So most adults assume that they will lie down on the couch on their backs. But some analysands are hesitant, even afraid to use the couch. There are different reasons why this might be and after a few minutes or sessions it will usually be addressed by the analysand or the analyst. It is not imperative to use the couch if you are in analysis, but it is thought to be beneficial. On the couch, it is felt to reassure most analysands that they will not act on their impulses, e.g., hostile or sexual, and it helps them feel safer. Using the couch and not seeing the analyst behind you is believed to support a *controlled regression*. This is believed to happen because the analysand"s attention is turned inward and the pull of childhood "fixation points" leads to past memories, feelings and attitudes. Despite this regression, when the adult walks out of the consulting room he or she resumes more adult viewpoints and behavior. Analysands are chosen to benefit from psychoanalysis because they have the "ego strength" to deal with such regression. For some, the couch is like a bed and to engage in exploring sexual fantasies with another person is stimulating of erotic feelings.

Laying on one's back with your eyes looking at the ceiling or closed is also felt to encourage getting in touch with your thoughts and/or feelings insofar as you are not distracted as much by other things around you, including the analyst's face. Of course, for those analysands who are hesitant to use the couch until they feel safer, the process of analyzing fears may ultimately allow him or her to try using the couch. Some who cannot use the couch to begin with may agree to turn the chair so they are still sitting up but not facing the analyst. Some analysands close their eyes on the couch, others may not, some cross their legs, some turn their heads to occasionally look at a clock if there is one they can see from their position on the couch, others look at a wrist watch, some speak very softly, some might even turn to look at the analyst behind them, etc. All these behaviors have meaning but may not be understood for a while. Analysts must be comfortable with "not knowing," with *tolerating ambiguity*.

Then there is the issue of the so-called "basic rule," *free association*. That it is called a "rule" is a misnomer; it is more a recommendation. Some analysts elect to state the idea of free association from the beginning, as I do, thinking that analysands need some education about a process they have never encountered and unique as a form of communication.

The basic rule suggests that analysands try to allow themselves to verbalize all of their thoughts, images, fantasies and feelings without censorship as they emerge into their conscious mind, not to willfully think of things to talk about. The analyst acknowledges that this is an ideal insofar as at times there will be a reluctance to do so, but that also is encouraged to be acknowledged verbally. The analyst acknowledges that being told "this is a place where you can say **anything**" is probably the only time in one's life to hear this and it runs counter to everyday experience. The aim is to become more comfortable with one's mind and to eventually appreciate how the mind works. Incidentally, psychoanalysis as a therapeutic technique is interested in the mind and not the brain.

While free association is an ideal, it does not mean that the analysand is busy doing this and the analyst is silent most of the time. Certainly silence is a technical strategy that is useful to give an analysand the opportunity to reflect on thoughts and images. This does not mean that verbal dialogue between analyst and analysand does not take place. Often there is verbal interaction between the two. Analysts may ask a question, or an analysand may respond to an interpretation with a question or an association that takes the analytic material to a deeper level. Sometimes it may seem that the analytic process with adults is a "verbal playground." Metaphors may be spoken of, and even a joke may be told to get a point across.

Akin to the "basic rule" for the analysand is one for the analyst, although it is not called a "rule." The analyst is expected to remain *neutral* to the analysand's material and to adhere to *abstinence* and not gratification with regard to the wishes of the analysand. I will have more to say about this when I discuss the Limits that exist in the analytic process.

With adolescents the basic rule can also be stated as an ideal. I say "ideal" because analysts know that it can be sought after but rarely if ever fully achieved. This is because of how the mind seeks pleasure and avoids unpleasure. This is a universal human characteristic. Free association will be interrupted when a part of the mind we call the Ego senses unpleasure in the form of anxiety, guilt, shame, embarrassment, etc. At that point analysands will more actively think of something else to say other than what made them uncomfortable.

The basic principle in beginning an analysis is to enable the analysand regardless of their age to feel safe. This is especially essential in psychoanalytic work with young children. The analyst being an adult is believed, for the most part, by a child to be helpful and protective. Of course, with those children who have been traumatized by adults the expectation has to be gradually experienced by the child to feel safe. Children do not verbally free associate; they are incapable of doing so because of a de-emphasis on words and a natural tendency to act. Some child analysts look upon a sequence of play as free association. Many believe it is not insofar as play and its sequence is limited often by the properties of the toy being utilized or the rules of the game. For a child to voluntarily discard the controls of action, as in free association where non-control over sequences of thoughts put into words is sought, if achieved could lead many children to destructive actions. Such experiences run counter to enabling children to feel safe.

With time the child analyst helps the young child feel safe by his or her verbal interventions that convey to the child that they are welcomed and accepted, that the child has a mind that contains thoughts and feelings which can be understood. The child eventually grasps that the adult child analyst he is playing with also has a mind with thought and feelings that may be like his or her own but could also be different. We call this "mindfulness," a process instilled in most infants early on in their interactions with an empathic mother.

Establishing a Working Alliance

The efforts of a psychoanalyst to establish a working alliance with analysands of all ages, I think, is foremost in their minds in the beginning of the analysis, the early stage. Why is it so important? It is so because one wants the analysand as an ally, someone who has an initial curiosity about how the mind works so improvements can be made upon solutions to mental conflict. The aim is to strengthen this beginning curiosity so that it will help the analysand to withstand internal pressures to abandon the process once it deepens and unpleasant feelings are encountered. However, I wish to underscore, that interventions aimed at reinforcing the working alliance continue until the last day of an analysis. In a final session there might be an occasion for the analyst to support his departing analysand's comments that they are hopeful they can continue the work of analysis independently, i.e., the analyst may support the identification with the analyzing function of the analyst.

A working alliance is possible with the evolving and expanding capacity of the analysand to both "observe" and "experience" the world and the Self. These critical cognitive capacities are more developed in adults compared to adolescents and younger children. Because of limited cognitive capacities that limit ability to understand the Self and the world, *insight* potentially is not as thorough in young children. By mid-adolescence with the beginning of more abstract thinking, they, too, are capable of tolerating and being evaluative of their mental contents. With younger children, interpretations can be taken sometimes as permission to enact a heretofore forbidden impulse. So, the child analyst must be cognizant of the young analysand's capacity to control his or her desires. The structure of a child's mind may not have developed or stabilized sufficiently so that bringing awareness to an impulse, if expressed, could increase anxiety.

In working with adults, analysts soon recognize that many of the issues their analysands are dealing with originated during their childhoods. After awhile adults have insight into this as the origin of their discomfort. An intervention aimed at strengthening the working alliance is to get across to the adult that he or she will have the capacity to help one's inner child grow up to be more adult. Adult patients appreciate that the analytic process is supportive of this aim.

In working with adolescents and younger children it is imperative that the analyst establishes a working alliance with their parents. It is the parents who will be confronted by their child's threats not to continue their treatment when "the going gets tough," i.e., when the child starts to experience discomfort because of the uncovering of conflicts in analysis. The parents at that moment need to be empathic with their child's struggle and support the value of continuing by supplying hope that things will get better in the future with continued analysis. With some parents and some adults at the time of the recommendation for analysis it may be helpful to point out that there may come a time when their child or they may feel better and they may think it is time to stop, but they will be mistaken.

In psychoanalytic treatment of analysands of all ages, an important idea to point out to all is that there is a distinction between "thoughts" and "deeds." It does not seem to matter to people, even those who are not religiously observant, that the difference matters. If you have a "bad" thought or fantasy, you should feel as guilty as if you enacted it. As a psychoanalyst, if you can help those you see to appreciate the distinction, the working alliance is strengthened. In recent times women have come forth to accuse men in past or present positions of power over them to have sexually harassed or abused them. Sometimes a period of time has elapsed between the time of the assault and the time of the public accusation by a woman. Often the woman will talk about "shame", as if the assault or harassment was her fault. Objectively, these women need not feel ashamed. It occurs, regretfully, because many women feel that if they have desired to be noticed by a man it is their fault if a man acts like a predator. I believe these women lose the distinction between a "wish" and a "want." A childhood wish to be desired by one's father likely originated during the Oedipal years, universal in Western culture, but this is not the same as "wanting" to be assaulted.

If guilt is lessened then analysands will more likely share their private thoughts with their analysts. A private thought or fantasy does not hurt another human you may even care for. One can try to understand its derivation and learn about oneself, maybe even forgive oneself and open oneself up to be more compassionate and forgiving of others.

Young *preoedipal* children often experience conflict essentially with the external world. Their own defensiveness about wishes perceived to be unacceptable to external authority makes it difficult to establish an alliance with the child analyst. It feels scary to be curious about their own minds and their role in conflict. But it does occur with some precocious children.

Resistance

Resistance in my view and that of a majority of psychoanalysts is a basic characteristic of the human mind. It is an outcome of the mind seeking pleasure and avoiding unpleasure. For example, we avoid saying things all the time in social situations if we think a recipient will be disturbed by our utterance, or we put some thought out of our mind if we think it is salacious. When this mental process occurs in the consulting room we refer to the defensive maneuver as resistance.

With our analysands we might notice a silence or a change of topic after they have said something connected to intense feeling, e.g., sadness, anger or excitement. They may have a "slip of the tongue" (a parapraxis) but ignore it, or they may be speaking of something in the present but suddenly shift to the past. Often we may make a verbal intervention but their response is apparently unrelated, without acknowledgment of this. When analysts notice this, (*close processing analysis*) they suspect that a resistance has occurred and they often choose to bring it to the analysand's attention if it goes unmentioned. The aim in making a resistance interpretation is to raise the analysand's curiosity about his or her mind and to evoke the working alliance. We hope the analysand will be able to identify the unpleasant feeling, often anxiety, that prompted the resistance, and express what the danger was that was imagined if a particular mental content was not avoided.

In addition to silence after an intervention by the analyst, resistance can take myriad forms. Joking frequently might suggest resistance. We do not expect analysands to lose their sense of humor, but if it is excessively employed an analyst might wonder if topics that elicit *dysphoric* feelings (depressive) are being avoided.

The analyst might say, "Have you noticed that you often tell jokes or laugh readily at things I say?" Another common form of resistance is forgetting of dreams. Dreaming is universal and if analysands do not bring theirs into analysis it likely has to do with resistance. Again, the analyst will wonder if the analysand has noticed that he or she almost never brings in a dream into analysis. If the analysand agrees the analyst might wonder, "Why do you think that is?" This could lead to analysis of resistance.

It is important that the analyst avoids being combative with the analysand. The analyst keeps in mind the ubiquity of resistance; the human mind seeks pleasure and avoids "unpleasure." The presence of resistance does not mean the analysand is a poor candidate for psychoanalysis.

Secrets are often kept out of an analysis until the analysand feels safe and trusting of the analyst. The basic premise of psychoanalytic treatment is that the analysand agrees to say whatever enters their mind; there can be no exception that an analyst can agree to. If the analysand discloses that they have *suppressed* a secret the analyst will acknowledge that it is progress that they disclosed this and it is important that they talk about it when they feel more comfortable doing so, because a secret can play an important role in their mental life.

Avoidance of certain topics is another sign of resistance. For example, the topic of sexual desire may not be brought up by an adult, masturbation by an adolescent, eating issues by an analysand suffering from an eating disorder, the death of a pet guinea pig by a child who does not want to feel grief, etc. An analyst will point out the absence of ubiquitous topics, or the absence of a topic that almost always follows a particular life experience, and try to raise the analysand's curiosity about the absence.

Avoidance of curiosity about the analyst is a frequent resistance. When this is eventually pointed out after some time has passed, many adults will say that they thought it was off-limits to express such thoughts. The analyst will remind them that they have been advised that they "can say anything" which would include thoughts about their analyst. One might add that such thoughts can help the process insofar as other content could emerge to further the analysis. This will make sense to many adult analysands but there will remain some where this remains a strong resistance. Adolescents and younger children sometimes can be quite vocal about their view of their analysts.

The enactment of a resistance occurs in analysands of all ages. With adults and adolescents it is most often verbal insofar as this is the way they express themselves. With younger children it is mostly in the form of action insofar as this is the way they mostly express themselves. The resistance occurs in their play. For example, the topic of the play changes after something is enacted that expresses a lot of feeling in the play, perhaps verbally (a shout) or in an impulse (something thrown), and the child does not appear to acknowledge it. With children, resistance is sometimes very overt, e.g., running out of the room, and with adolescents (and adults) it often takes the form of coming late or not showing up for a session.

With adolescents, they usually avoid the topic of masturbation. It is not an activity that they volunteer and speak freely about. This is in part an internalization of cultural mores about the topic, although over the years I have seen a greater normalization of the activity. Masturbation was once thought to be a sign of pathology but is now accepted by Western culture as universal, but still something you do privately and do not talk about. Young children of both genders touch their genitals and experience pleasure. If parents notice this, most do not chastise the child but do say they should do it only in the privacy of the bedroom. Of course, there are still parents who shame a child caught masturbating. If an adolescent can talk about the act of masturbation and the accompanying fantasy, a child analyst can reassure the adolescent that it is normal. Analysis of the fantasy can help the adolescent have a sense of normalcy about their sexual desire. Resistance is often encountered because of shame and guilt. Sometimes excessive masturbation is a sign of anxiety about interacting with the opposite sex. Overcoming resistance about the topic can lead to the open admission of such anxiety.

Another topic that analysts encounter in contemporary times with evidence of resistance, but less than a decade ago, is the topic of *sexual gender*. We used to think this was pretty much fixed by three years of age, but now we believe gender assignment is more fluid. Adolescents are more comfortable about the issue and some, albeit with much pain and social ostracism, declare they have adopted the gender identity opposite from the one they were born with. Overcoming resistance about talking about their intentions or conflicts allows analytic intervention to be of benefit to these adolescents.

The human mind employs many different processes of avoiding unpleasure. We call these processes *defense mechanisms.* The part of the mind that employs them we call the Ego. In our psychoanalytic model of the mind, the ego is the mental "structure" that carries out "executive functions," rational thinking, judgment, memory, reality testing, and defensive processes to eliminate unpleasure (e.g., feeling of anxiety, guilt, shame, embarrassment, etc.)

Insofar as our focus is on technique I will only summarily refer below to some typical mechanisms of defense, but keep in mind that the ego is resourceful and can use any mental process, thought or action, defensively to ward off unpleasant feelings.

Signal anxiety is a special feeling employed by the ego to warn a person (the Self) that either a real or imagined danger threatens the person. The danger will be experienced if a forbidden wish or its derivative is expressed in action. If the danger is felt to be in the internal world it could be condemnation by or loss of love from the superego (guilt) or in the external world some sort of punishment (loss of the object [abandonment], loss of the object's love, castra-tion [some physical harm]. To avoid the danger the forbidden wish must be modified to be less unacceptable to the imagined or real source of the danger. Here is when defenses are called into play and the modified wish if expressed is a "compromise" reflecting aspects of the derivative wish and the defensive modifications. So instead of pummeling a younger sibling you shout that he "stinks and should be thrown away." If the defensive maneuvers are not sufficient the signal anxiety can change to *panic*, with accompanying feeling of helplessness and feeling overwhelmed.

Repression is the permanent exclusion of thoughts and feelings from consciousness and assigning them to the unconscious part of the mind. It is "the Mother of all defenses!" *Suppression* is the conscious decision not to talk about something. *Reaction formation* is when the opposite is expressed from what is meant, e.g., an expression of loving feelings when what are felt by the doer is hateful feelings, or vice versa, towards the recipient. *Projection* is when a wish or thought or feeling towards someone is felt or believed to be directed instead towards you. *Externization* occurs when unwanted aspects of the Self are attributed to others. For example, "He is greedy and exploitative of others," said by someone who typifies such a person. *Denial* is when someone ignores completely a bit of reality and acts without taking into account the reality in their decision-making. *Negation* Is when a wish or thought is allowed access to consciousness and verbalized by an analysand but negated. For example, " I have no sexual feelings for my teacher." An analyst will point out, "Who said you did?" bringing the analysand's atten-tion to the defensive maneuver. *Rationalization* is when a person evades feeling guilty by fabricating a rational reason for their action. *Displacement* is when someone expresses a wish towards someone safer other than the person it was intended for originally. *Dissocia-tion* is in a different category from the above defenses insofar as it is not directed at a particular thought, wish, or feeling, but at the Self. The person is so uncomfortable "being in their own skin" that they psychologically feel apart from himself or herself. *Isolation of affect* occurs when an idea or thought is expressed devoid of the accompanying affect connected to it. It is akin to *intellectualization* wherein an analysand narrates the meaning of an experience with "academic" understanding devoid of feeling. *Reversal of affect* occurs when the opposite feeling is reported from what is being experienced.

Resistance is reduced when there is a strong working alliance between the analysand and the analyst, but it is never eliminated. As mentioned earlier, with young children, in addition to endeavoring to establish a working alliance of sorts with them, a result less achievable because of their greater intolerance for unpleasant feelings, the analyst works at establishing one with their parents.

There are some defenses that have been employed since childhood and have proven effective in reducing anxiety. After awhile they are utilized regularly and become *character* defenses. We all have character styles that we "automatically" use to reduce expectations of anxiety producing situations. They become "firewalls" against expected danger. For example, procrastination, over-optimism, clowning, excessive cynicism, etc., are all example of character styles. Often character defenses are based on identification with primary people in childhood, such as parents.

Transference

As I understand psychoanalysis as a clinical technique, *transference* is another major feature of the unfolding dynamics. Transference occurs when a past relationship Is re-experienced in a contemporary relationship with another person different from the one with whom it originated. Consciously, the person enacting the transference is not aware, in most instances, of the re-experience of feelings and thoughts, and instead believes they have a contemporary origin. This is possible, psychoanalysts believe, because the *Unconscious* is timeless. That is, memories and accompanying feelings when re-experienced consciously, feel as if they are contemporary. This re-experiencing is a part of everyone's life. For example, we may experience a male teacher with the same thoughts and feelings that we once had with our father but not be aware of this consciously. In some instances we may have a thought, "He's a lot like Dad." When this experience occurs in the consulting room we call it transference. The analyst is now reacted towards, without awareness, as if they are the person from the past. We speak of *positive transference* and *negative transference*. "Positive" has to do with loving wishes and feelings, while "negative" refers to angry wishes and hateful feelings.

At the beginning of an analysis before a strong working alliance has taken hold, it can be positive transference feelings that may prevent an analysand from a premature termination. There are instances when a positive transference can have a non-beneficial effect. Sometimes it leads an analysand to be compliant with the analyst's interpretations, not thoughtfully considering its merits and noticing the feelings that are evoked, but rather simply agreeing that it is correct to please the analyst. It could be also a way to avoid examining the material further because of anxiety. The analyst with such an analysand needs to be self-aware, too, that they are not making comments with an authoritarian tone that scares an analysand who uses passivity as a defense against being assertive.

There is also the rare so-called *transference cure.* Here a patient may feel "cured" after a few consultations prior to entering analysis, or very early in the analysis. Symptoms have gone and he or she feels better. There is no need to continue. I understand this as an unconscious idealization of the analyst as omniscient, coupled with unconscious resistance to undergo analysis.

Transference can occur with analysands of all ages but is less frequent the younger the child. This is because the young child is still very invested in and involved with contemporary people such as parents in the here-and-now. These contemporary feelings may be re-experienced with the child analyst but we do not consider them transference. We consider this type of relationship a *displacement* from the parents. (Below we will discuss the different types of relationships a child experiences with their analyst.)

Transference is a valuable component of the analytic process insofar as its occurrence is thought of as a "window into the past," allowing the analyst to understand the analysand's evolution. Eventually, when the analyst engages in pointing out the origin of thoughts and feelings and begins to make interventions in the form of interpretations, the analysand gradually gets a better emotional understanding of himself or herself and the origin of conflicts. Initially, an analyst will not immediately bring the attention of the analysand to a past relationship when transference is suspected. This is because we want the intensity of the relationship experienced by the analysand towards the analyst to build up and intensify. At what point the analyst inquires about a past relationship differs with each analysand. We do not want understanding to be only intellectual but also emotional. Basically, though it depends on the working alliance and if the intensity of the relationship has begun to be fraught with such intense feelings and wishes that a feeling of safety for the analysand begins to be in jeopardy. It is then felt that an analysand will emotionally understand that there is a history to what they are currently feeling, and it makes sense.

Adolescents have to deal with pubertal changes. This causes a focus on their body. Early in childhood the mother, usually, is felt to be the "owner" of one's body. Gradually in late latency children start to take ownership of their body. When puberty "hits" many adolescents feel overwhelmed and regress in their object relatedness, at least internally. The mother is now expected again to be in charge of their body and she is blamed for the "noxious" bodily changes they are supposed to be in "charge" of but feel over whelmed by because of bodily sexual urges. Such adolescent analysands will develop a maternal transference to the analyst, feeling both the unwilling victim of the analyst but also wishing the analyst to take charge. Resistance often is expressed in 'missed" sessions, a common event in work with this age group in analysis.

In some instances, most often when the genders of the analytic couple are opposite, an *eroticized transference* can occur. The analysand will be seductive, coquettish, and is interested in a receptive response from the analyst. When this is not forthcoming, but instead the analyst responds in an empathic, compassionate, and professional manner, the analysand will feel rejected, frustrated and angry. Hopefully, the transference can be analyzed and insight gained. In instances of an erotic transference, the analyst needs to be sensitive to their own erotic feelings so that he or she does not enter into an *enactment* (discussed later) with the analysand.

Sometimes, an erotic transference can be disguised by an analysand's preoccupation with one's body, often seeming hypochondriacal, i.e., an excessive worry about the health of the body, imagining all sorts of ailments. In this manner, the analysand brings the analyst's attention to one's body.

With adult analysands particularly, and less often with adolescents, and only occasionally with young children, a *transference neurosis* may occur. This happens when the transference gets so intense it becomes the primary relationship for the analysand. It is in this relationship, then, that the analysand seeks gratifications, feels loved or unloved and expects praise or criticism. Conflicts with significant people lessen, and symptoms (neurotic solutions to conflicts) lessen. When the analysand is in the midst of the transference neurosis, again, it is an opportunity for the analyst and analysand to gain insight into the origin of personal conflicts and to gain emotional *insight*. At the height of a transference neurosis the analysand does not seek insight but rather seeks gratification. With interpretations, gradually the intensity of the transference neurosis diminishes and the analyst is no longer "all-important" as during its height. Adolescents are still involved with present day people as are children, even more so, which runs counter to the development of a transference neurosis. Hence, with these age groups, particularly young children, transference neuroses are rare. *Character transference* is what an analysand brings to the analysis from the very beginning. It does not gradually develop.

Real Object, Developmental Object, & Transference Object

In psychoanalytic theory we talk of a person as a "self" and of the person they are relating to as an "object." We do this not to objectify or dehumanize the "other" but in the interests of clarity to distinguish the two people. We have talked above about transference. The analyst in a transference relationship with an analysand is referred to as a *transference object*. As indicated above, patients of all ages are capable of responding to their analyst in this way, although the incidence typically decreases the younger the analysand. We also refer to an analyst as being a *developmental object*. Analysands of all ages may experience their analyst in this manner. When this happens the analyst has responded to the analysand in a growth promoting way compensating for an experience that the analysand has been deprived of in their earlier years, probably because of an absent parent or a disturbed caretaker. As an infant or very young child, an adult caretaker serves as an auxiliary ego providing the immature child in their charge with the cognitive or emotional support the child lacks. In some instances, noted above, this may not happen. The analyst by analyzing may provide the experience that they lacked. This experience is not a deliberate strategy and the analysand has a "second chance," so to speak, to take advantage of this growth promoting experience. The analyst has been used as a developmental object.

All analysands, irrespective of age, but predominantly by young children, may also experience the analyst as a *real object*. Young children are used to seeing adults as caretakers, and their expectation is that the child analyst will be so too. There are innumerable ways in which this manifests itself. For example, the child analyst may assist the child is maneuvering a heavy object, such as a door or table, or reaching a light switch that is above the child's reach, etc. Analysts know that they cannot be robots and only be in an interpretive mode. Hence, there are innumerable times when they say things that are real, like "Thank you," "My condolences on the death of your mother," "I hope your surgical procedure goes well," etc. Analysands of all ages appreciate this humane treatment, and it does not interfere with the analyst becoming a transference object, unless it is excessive in frequency.

Analysts are like all people and sometimes they make mistakes. I think it is best to admit the mistake if it affects an analysand. For example, I confused the return date from a vacation with the return to work date and scheduled appointments on the day of my return, which was in the evening. I telephoned the people affected, apologized for my confusion and offered to reschedule if it was convenient for them with no obligation for them to do so. I noticed no adverse effects on their treatment. I think if we expect analysands to be truthful, analysts need to be so too if it is not believed to be a burden on analysands. I introduce the latter idea because I think to share some personal events in the analyst's life with analysands can be burdensome and ought not be done. For example, a surgical procedure undergone during the analyst's vacation need not be talked about if the expectation is that the analyst will not need to cancel sessions. Also, it may be that the need for surgery or the result of it will not even be noticeable. A life event like an analyst's child's marriage or a grandchild's birth ought not be shared unless the analysand, for some reason, becomes aware of it. Then the reactions of the analysand can be analyzed.

Countertransference

Psychoanalysts are human and being so like everyone else they have "hot spots," personal issues that owe their origin to their personal life experiences. An essential part of training to become an analyst included a personal psychoanalysis. Having an emotional understanding of yourself and your emotional sensitivities will aid a clinical analyst in dealing with future patients. An analysand may bring up a topic that is a sensitive one for their analyst. The analyst may not be initially aware that they are responding to the material in a non-helpful way. They may be silent, have an angry tone, change the focus by their intervention, feel excited by the material and seductively encourage further details by their manner and words, etc. The above may also not be noticed initially by the analysand. We speak of the interaction at this point as an *enactment*. Eventually, hopefully, one of the two will notice and an analysand may comment about a change in the analyst's tone, for example, since she has brought up erotic fantasies about her male analyst. If brought to his attention, an analyst may agree to the observation. "I think your observation has merit and I will think more about it." In my experience if an analysand makes mention of an enactment, for me to acknowledge its likely presence, has always advanced the treatment in a positive way. Analysands like to hear confirmation that the analyst is human, not a robot, has an Unconscious too, and he or she can have an effect on the analyst. An analyst may note the change before their analysand, may not say something openly but may ponder the experience. If nothing is said, the analyst makes a judgment that the analysand may not benefit from an admission and may feel unsafe but will likely benefit from a change in the analyst's behavior. The analyst will undergo some self-analysis to gain more insight as to why they were effected so by the material. Another way that an analyst may unwittingly be affected by an analysand's material about a significant person in their past, is to behave in a manner that we call *role responsiveness.* Here the analyst unwittingly enacts the behavioral mode of the significant object from the past of the analysand. I understand it as an unconscious identification with the object, a form of countertransference.

It used to be thought that countertransference was always detrimental to a psychoanalysis, that the analyst should keep its occurrence to their self, and in some instances seek peer supervision or further personal analysis. This attitude has been changed so that now we believe that countertransference is inevitable and it can be useful in understanding not only oneself but also one's analysand. Most analysts are now not ashamed of having countertransference but think of it as a tool in their bag of technical "instruments."

Freud encouraged analysts to listen with "free floating attention." By this he meant they should allow their attention to go freely towards the analysand's associations and towards their own reveries in reaction to the analysand's material. In doing the latter an analyst who is tolerant of his or her own thoughts or images can be alert to uncomfortable feelings they may be experiencing while listening to their analysand's associations. Countertransference can then be analyzed. Analysts now accept that both their own personality and their theory influence interventions and consequently the shape of analysand's material.

An issue that is recent in psychoanalysis is "love." Can an analyst come to "love" his or her analysand? This will be asked or be implicit in analytic material. Often it arises after expressions of love are voiced from the couch and the analysand asks or it is implied that he or she is curious if the feeling is mutual. Analysts have been reluctant to answer this question. They have dealt with it with an analytic posture. "Notice you ask me this after professing your love for me. It took courage to tell me you love me, and it would be very hurtful to you if I did not tell you I feel love for you too. I am committed to your best interests and hope you achieve your goals.

If that isn't love then I don't know what is." The analyst who feels this way does love the analysand, but it is different from "romantic love" or "erotic love." In my opinion, either of the last two, if felt, would be countertransference and very burdensome to disclose to an analysand.

Interpretation

Another fundamental aspect of psychoanalytic treatment is the making of an interpretation. An interpretation is a verbal intervention that is meant to provide some modicum of insight that in turn will deepen the material, i.e., allow the analysand to access additional mental content heretofore repressed. Insight is sought. An interpretation based on the *topographic model* of the mind, makes conscious what was formerly unconscious. Based on the structural model of the mind, an interpretation expands the ego's understanding of some mental content unknown up to that point, albeit the site of feelings like anxiety and/or guilt associated with the repressed content. An interpretation is aimed at expanding an analysand's self-understanding, both intellectually and emotionally. It is also a way ultimately of helping an analysand reclaim a sense of *self-agency.* This is so because with greater tolerance of instinctual drive, an analysand gains a greater sense of control over their decision-making and actions in the real world.

An *interpretative process* is more than a declarative statement from the analyst. It may include clarifications, confrontations, questions, initial steps at working through, even supportive comments, all aimed at helping the analysand gain insight. Essentially the process describes a dialogue between the "analytic couple."

Analysts try to use vocabulary that is easily understood, not requiring a dictionary, and use words evocative of feeling, e.g., " scared" instead of "intimidated." The aim is to reach the scared "inner child' whom the analysand can help to feel safe to grow up. Such an intervention can be delivered to analysands of all ages.

An analyst does not want to take on an authoritarian manner so that an analysand feels that they are being lectured about what is right or wrong by an all-knowing authority. It is best to convey interpretations as conjectures so that the analysand does not feel lectured to and can feel comfortable to refute an interpretation. "I wonder if you may have been feeling…" Sometimes interpretations can be made in a playful way and the analysand responds back with a similar tone. "You're hoping Prince Charming will put the glass slipper on your foot." "Yes, but with my luck the shoe probably will be a size too big."

An analyst does not make interpretations from the start. One waits until there is confidence about the meaning of material being brought by the analysand. The analyst is hopeful that an analysand will be curious about the workings of their mind. If made too soon, an interpretation could increase resistance. A general principal in making interpretations is to work from the *surface* to the *depth*. The analyst judges the analysand's readiness to hear an interpretation. Usually, both analyst and analysand are aware of the uncomfortable feelings of the surface content.

From the above you can understand that the readiness is based on the strength of the working alliance, the intensity of resistance, and the quality of the transference. The weakened intensity of the resistance will bring attention to mental content that at the moment has the most affect attached to it. It is the mental content at this surface that the analyst will judge to be most ready to be interpreted. This is a strategic technical choice. An interpretation when made by an analyst carries the hopeful expectation that the analysand will be identified with the *analyzing function* of the analyst.

For example, the analyst might say, "You seem to be uncomfortable, judging from your silence, about what I just said about your apparent discomfort being invited to your parents' home for Thanksgiving." This interpretation is meant to bring attention to defensiveness about conflicted feelings and thoughts about the invitation. An intervention might be, "I wonder if what I just said about your attitude towards attending a family reunion is reminiscent of what your father might say?" Such an interpretation is meant to bring attention to transference feelings and thoughts that could be elaborated upon by the analysand. Some interpretations underscore a feeling evidenced by the analysand. A question might be asked, "What are you feeling about what you just said?" Naming a feeling often will allow the associated thought to be brought into consciousness and to be felt and connected thoughts to be verbalized.

With adolescents, the same judgment used with an adult, is employed as to timing of an interpretation. It might be said, "Your account of your noticing the girl sitting at the desk across from you suggests that you felt excited because of the physical closeness of such a sexy girl." The analyst notices the adolescent recognizes his excitement but is uneasy about it. This interpretation to an adolescent is meant to bring his attention to sexual feelings and to convey he can talk here about anything he chooses to. Or, "Do you notice that your attendance here has become more irregular ever since I commented about your conflicted desires to masturbate?" The aim here is to underscore the adolescent's struggles with masturbation, with the hopeful expectation that he might feel less inclined to keep it a secret. There is the *act of masturbation* and the accompanying *masturbation fantasy*. The latter can tell both the analyst and the analysand a lot about the status of the sexual drive, its psychosexual level and its aim, if it can be examined analytically. Noting the adolescent's anxiety and offering the empathic intervention that the act is universal may allow further exploration.

An interpretation is aimed at the Ego, although all mental structures, such as the Superego and Id will be affected too because of the *multiple determination* of mental conflict. What this refers to is how complex mental processes can be and how many structures of the mind can have in-put. For example, if there is a wish to pull the pony tail of the girl sitting in front of you in the fourth grade of elementary school, you may feel anxiety because the hostile/sadistic wish (Id), is opposed by your conscience that lets you know it is not a "nice" thing to do (Superego), and you know that the girl may yell out and the teacher will get involved and you may be punished (Ego).

There are some interpretations that are *reconstructions* of past experiences that influence the present world view of the analysand. For example, "I get the impression that your view of how men and women deal with one another so that men are dominant and women are submissive may be based on how your father controlled your mother." Reconstructions are based on a psychoanalytic tenet of human dynamics that contends that unless you understand the past it repeats itself in the present. Reconstructive interpretations with young children seem to be less used insofar as they are more involved and influenced by present external and internal reality.

Reconstructive interpretations are used with analysands who have been traumatized in the past. *Trauma* occurs when an individual is unprepared for some experience that scares them immensely so that the ego feels **overwhelmed and helpless**. With the passing of time this terrible experience may be repressed or the individual dissociates from any derivative of the memory so it is as if it never happened. A gap in memory results from trauma. When helping adult and adolescent analysands to process the trauma it occurs to the analyst that the memory may be fact or may be a fantasy. Freud originally thought that hysterical woman often were seduced by their fathers but later came to recognize that this was a fantasy that satisfied a libidinal wish. Eventually, with analytic processing of the trauma, what is referred to as *working through,* one becomes more confidant that the trauma happened or that it was a fantasy. It can be difficult sometimes to distinguish the two because of the use of denial by the victim and the perpetrator. It is significant to distinguish one from the other because it is therapeutic for the traumatized individual to confront the perpetrator of the abuse. With young children who have been traumatized it may be necessary to confront the perpetrator(s) or remove the child from the home temporarily or permanently until the parents can be worked with and change their parenting. For example, some parents believe it is good for young children to be exposed to nudity or even to witness sexual intercourse. They believe it makes the child more comfortable "within their own skin," and to accept their sexuality. This rationaliza-tion covers pathological *exhibitionism*. It is not in the best interests of young children to be exposed to parental nudity or to sexual intimacy (*primal scene*). It is too exciting to a child to be constantly observing parental nudity (cumulative trauma) and the child has no way to discharge the feelings. A young child, also, may interpret the sounds emanating from the parental couple during sexual intimacy as the sounds of one parent beating the other.

Analysts do not only make reconstructions of the past; analysands also may reconstruct the past as they gain insight. Also, more than one revision may take place as resistance is weakened, insight is gained, and more unconscious memories are allowed into consciousness.

The traumatized individual sometimes employs a *screen memory* defensively. A screen memory is a memory of something that happened but without the traumatic quality. For example, a memory of two dogs copulating may be a screen to cover over the anxious memory of witnessing the primal scene.

Children experience some traumas that are avoidable and some that are not. Some traumas happen once, *shock traumas*, some happen more than once over stretches of time, *cumulative traumas*. Child abuse, either physical or emotional, sexual molestation, exposure to parental sexual intercourse are examples of cumulative trauma. The death of a parent or beloved grandparent, being bitten by a dog, having unplanned emergency surgery, are examples of shock trauma.

In some instances a trauma experienced may be a danger that is in synchrony with the psychosexual phase that is ongoing at the time of the experience. For example, surgery during the phallic phase may be experienced as castration. This could strengthen the trauma or cause a regression. A traumatic experience could result in disruption of progressive development. In child analysis, it is important to help the traumatized child to work through the trauma so that progressive development is not hampered.

In some instances, the cause of a behavior might have a physiological origin, but, nevertheless, the meaning of the behavior may be psychological. We endeavor to make this distinction clear to our analysands. The skeptical analysand might comment, "Sometimes a cigar is a cigar." Here the "meaning" of reference to a cigar is being noted. What I have in mind is different. For example, an adult male analysand might need to interrupt sessions a couple of times to urinate. While the cause of this might be a benign enlarged prostate or some drink ingested prior to the session, a physiological determinant, the meaning may be psychological. The meaning, however, based on the dynamics of the analysand and the timing of the interruptions can be the analysand's way of reassuring himself that his penis is still intact after experiencing *castration anxiety* on the couch, in the transference.

With analysands who are depressed it is important to discern if the depression is biological (*endogenous*) or reactive (*exogenous*). The latter refers to those occasions when someone has a normal grief reaction if someone you care for dies or if you are disappointed about the outcome of some event that you are very committed to. This is normal and not pathological; analysands will benefit from this being interpreted. We now know that women experiencing miscarriage have lots of grief that needs processing. It used to be believed that the best remedy would be for another pregnancy soon thereafter. A *replacement child* was thought to be a good way to deal with the earlier loss. Now we appreciate that the grief needs to be felt and processed. Replacement children are also burdened with issues of identity confusion; are they who they are or someone else who once was?

Another example is distinguishing between *normal guilt* and *neurotic guilt*. When one does not live up to an ideal then it is normal to feel guilty. In neurotic guilt one feels guilty about something they fantasized and did not act upon. An interpretation aimed at helping them to understand the difference between a fantasy or a wish and an act is helpful. An example of normal guilt might be a woman dealing with postpartum depression who feels guilty she has not been attentive to her newborn infant. This is normal guilt insofar as she has the ideal of caring for her offspring but could not because of a biological condition she had no control over. She can be helped by an interpretation that is aimed at relieving her of neurotic guilt.

With children, it is sometimes useful to make an interpretation about an imaginary child in order to allow it to be listened to. For example, "I once knew a boy named Johnny who always said "Yes" when he meant "No," because he was afraid an adult would not like him unless he did whatever he was told to do." In this manner a young child might understand the defense of reaction formation. He might follow this up with a belligerent comment that he does not like to be told what to do, opening up a new topic for discussion. Or a child analyst might say, "Ugh, that was hard." This simple expression of displeasure might allow a child to openly express similar degrees of distaste.

With adolescents, becoming more independent from parents is a developmental need. Severance from parents is not beneficial but more autonomy and confidence about it is beneficial for adolescents. For a while they may feel lonely, feeling bereft because of the diminished intensity of involvement from the real and *"inner"* *(below)* parents. We call this the *second individuation phase*, the first one occurs when the young child has *internalized* the caregiving parent. Doing so, they achieve *object constancy*, experiencing comfort and attachment from the internalized parent *imago*. This is a subjective sense of parents being within one-self. The toddler now can walk away and separate from the mother and not experience intense separation anxiety. Much interpretive work with adolescents is to help them to process feelings of insecurity about increased autonomy from parents. Often support is obtained from being a member of a group of other adolescents. Sometimes the choice of a group might involve joining an anti-social one and acts of delinquency need to be addressed by the analyst.

With the advent of puberty, many adolescents have a difficult time. They must come to terms with a new body image that integrates a mature sexual body with a body image that prior to puberty did not include the capacity to be a mother or father. The body image now is a sexual body image that often feels to them to be uncontrollable. There is an urge to masturbate. The urge can be very strong. The *central masturbation fantasy* must integrate childhood immature fantasies that seem "out of tune" with a mature sexual identity. This conflict affects all of the structures of the mind, the Id, Superego, and Ego. Freud postulated that the Ego is first and foremost a "body ego" suggesting the need to regulate bodily needs. It is this conundrum of feelings, desires and conflict that an adolescent analysand often presents to the analyst. With time, and the adolescent feeling safe, conflicts about their sexual body, gender identity, and their masturbation fantasy may be brought into analysis. The latter will be a mixture of past neurotic compromises and present day solutions.

Interpretation of the central masturbation fantasy will be gradual and reconstruction of the past antecedents integrated into the current adolescent fantasy will need to wait until the adolescent feels less anxious and more in control of sexual urges. Otherwise the adolescent might retreat from their contemporary conflicts about sexual expression and resist further efforts to deal with pubertal upheavals.

Analysis of identifications must take into account that the analysand's perception of the person identified with might not be valid. Careful analysis might help the analysand distinguish what was so and what they wished was so. Sometimes *identification with a perceived aggressor* takes place, and the analysand can process this and be reassured that they are capable of *dis-identifying* with this person. Also, an analysand who has been "wronged" by a significant figure from the past, such as a parent, with whom they feel estranged from, can consider through interpretations that the parent may have some redeemable features too.

Two other verbal interventions, not considered interpretations, are *clarification* and *confrontation*. Clarification occurs when an analyst is confused about something said and asks a question for greater clarity. For example, "Why is it you just said Jane is not a sibling although in the past you've included her as one." The analysand might respond, "That's because she is only a half-sibling and doesn't count." Of course, this could lead to further inquiry. Confrontation in common usage refers to an angry interaction, but that is not meant here. I use confrontation when an analysand is using denial and I have a sense that the "bubble" of denial is strong and can only be burst by a confrontation. "Do you notice that you repeatedly act with resignation to many instances where your spouse is hurtful to you, telling yourself that she cannot change?" This type of intervention may help the analysand to reconsider their pessimistic conclusion about their spouse, and even to explore further their passivity vis-a--vis their spouse. Or one might say to an adolescent, "Have you considered the consequences of being involved with a group of delinquent boys?"

With *pre-latency* children, the child analyst must keep in mind that interpretations take into account the particular developmental level of the child. One doe not want to increase the child's anxiety beyond a level that they can cope with so as not to illicit a *regression*. One assesses if there are adequate defenses so the child will not respond with a *temper tantrum,* a form of *acting-in* that they cannot control.

The issue of how does an analyst know if the interpretation made is correct or incorrect is not easy to answer. If correct, the analyst may expect to see some change in the transference. The change might follow the meaning of the interpretation, e.g., after interpreting how the analysand as a child felt his father to be uninterested in his after-school activities, it might be noticed later in the session observations are made about the analyst's interest in a particular event, a movie, seen by the analysand. It might be said, then, "Unlike your father who seemed uninterested in your after-school activities, you notice my asking questions about the movie you saw. Perhaps, you wished your father to be more inquisitive about your interests?" Sometimes, if an interpretation is correct, associations are offered by the analysand that goes deeper into details about the topic of the interpretation. A wrong interpretation might elicit resistance. For example, after an interpretation, there is a long silence, or a change of topic, or an equivocation such as "I don't know about that." A complicating factor, however, is that a correct interpretation might elicit resistance. This is likely to happen if the interpretation was made "too soon," i.e., before the analysand is ready to hear it. In such situations, time usually clarifies the issue.

Acting Out

Acting out is a term that often is misused to describe behavior that is impulsive, but if properly used the term has another meaning. If strictly used, it describes behavior that is a transference manifestation that occurs outside the consulting room. An adult male analysand may have an angry memory involving their father about an incident involving a school project that he led that took place years earlier but it cannot be accessed because it is repressed. At work, unexpectedly he has an angry verbal outburst towards his male boss who in praising the efforts of the office staff in completing a project does not specifically mention his leadership. With analytic work soon thereafter, the analysand is able to process the incident and link it to the analyst whom he feels neglected to praise him when he related a recent success at work, and then remember the childhood memory.

It is not uncommon in the case of married adult analysands where the spouse who may or may not be in analysis themselves asks partners to tell them what transpires in his or her analysis. While the query may be motivated by good intentions for intimacy, it encourages a form of acting out insofar as in the retelling of a session feelings and thoughts belonging in the consulting room may get "lost."

The analysand is aware of his or her behavior, although the analysand does not label it as "acting out," but is unaware of its meaning. Therefore it can be considered a type of resistance. Violations of the frame are often expressions of negative transference, e.g., coming late or payment made after the agreed upon date for submission of a check. In general, it is easier for analysands to verbalize positive transference than negative transference. Erotized positive transference is often acted-in the transference, e.g., a female analysand wearing a "sexy" outfit to her session.

With adolescent and child analysands, acting out will follow the same dynamic sequence, namely, transference, resistance to the transference, reoccurrence of the transference to a person outside the consulting room, followed, perhaps, by a report of the unexpected event and analytic processing of it leading to insight.

As mentioned earlier, when talking about countertransference, enactments can be understood as a unique form of acting out by the analyst, at least until the time of the analyst's recognition of the transference to the analysand. The one major difference is that it occurs inside the consulting room, but it could be acted outside too.

Limit Setting

There are not many occasions where limits need to be set in adult analysis. Most adults accept the implicit limits put forth in discussing the "frame" of the analysis. Of course, violations of the parameters of the frame often occur, and the analyst will make verbal interventions that bring it to the analysand's attention, with the expectation that the incident will be processed. For example, if payment of the fee is late the analyst will notice when payment is received if the analysand does or does not remark about the late payment. " You haven't remarked about late payment." The analysand may come up with a simple explanation such as, "I forget. Sorry." Or, assuming they have established a working alliance and are curious about their behavior (mind), they may remark, "I wonder what it means that I was late in payment." There are myriad meanings that are possible, e.g., it might be understood as an expression of the current state of the transference. The analysand may feel the analyst to be "withholding," so he or she dispense a little of the same "medicine" to him.

Sometimes the analysand may invite the analyst to an event, performing perhaps in a play or as an instrumentalist in a concert. This can occur with analysands of all ages. The analyst may elect to indicate appreciation of the invitation but in his judgment it is in the best interests of the analysis not to confuse for the analysand the role of the analyst. With young children an analyst expresses appreciation for the invitation but declines pointing out that he or she and the child have a very special relationship unlike any other. The analyst is their "worry doctor" and a friend but not like other friends. They meet in the office and not away from it. In my experience, a child may be disappointed but having a 'special" kind of a friend is compensatory and acceptable.

In a small community, it may be that the analyst and analysand are in the same or overlapping social circles. Both may get invited to a small dinner party. At such an event, other guests may direct personal questions to the analyst within "ear shot" of the analysand. The analyst may feel that the answers could burden the analysand and interfere negatively in the analysis. Openly discussing this with the analysand is helpful and one of the two may elect to decline the invitation. If this happens often the two can decide to take turns in declining invitations.

Again, in a small community, the analyst's spouse may interact with his analysand, not knowing this because of confidentiality. I think if this happens it is the responsibility of the analysand to indicate that he or she is in analysis with the spouse so that an intimate conversation is "off limits." Another limit setting may occur when after experiencing intense stress and adult analysand may request a "hug" from the analyst when exiting from the consulting room. The analyst empathizing with the stressful condition of the analysand politely declines and expresses physical contact of this type could burden the relationship of the two.

Related to limit setting is the basic premise of *neutrality* and *abstinence* followed by the analyst. Strictly speaking, neutrality refers to the analyst "positioning" understanding equidistant from the Ego, Superego, and Id. What this means is that the analyst listens with an "open mind" trying to listen for the influence of all the structures of the mind on the material the analysand is bringing into a session. It is an appreciation of the over-determination of mental processes, content and conflict. The analyst prefers the role of observer and not participant. We know, however, being an observer affects the process being observed especially if human beings are involved.

Abstinence refers to the non-gratification of the wishes primarily expressed in the transference. This is **very** important insofar as the lack of gratification encourages the continued and deeper expression, i.e., formerly repressed, of thoughts, fantasies, wishes, feelings, and conflict. It also contributes to increased feelings of safety because even though the analysand wishes to gratify his or her repressed wishes, and not only understand them, such an occasion would lead to guilt and anxiety too.

As valuable and essential as the concept of abstinence is, it is more complicated than total adherence to the principle. With the widening scope of psychoanalysis applied to more than neurotic patients, there was recognition that these patients could not tolerate high degrees of frustration due to a lack of gratification. There are some situations when, I believe, the analyst does not engage beneficially in one hundred percent abstinence. These occasions are referred to as *parameters.*

Some analysts do not offer to shake hands before a vacation, while I do so. Also, some decline to wish a patient well before a surgical procedure, or to express condolences when a relative dies, or to say "Happy Birthday." They have conviction that this is being too much of a "real person" and being so will interfere with being a transference object. I do not accept this. My thinking is, as expressed earlier, the analyst must be humane is dealing with analysands in a thoughtful way and that this will not interfere with the transference. I used to never answer questions of analysands about my vacation destinations, but now I do so. If they know, some will still express regrets about the interruption and some may even dare to say in a disquised fashion that I do not enjoy myself. I think that as the analyst gets to know more about his analysand, he or she learns what the likely consequences might be for answering or declining to answer. Early on and maybe never is there one hundred percent confidence that you understand your analysand. As said more than once, the analyst must tolerate ambiguity. So, an analyst might apologize for misremembering a bit of family history. The analysand could understand an apology by the analyst means he or she does not tolerate anger. But then not to apologize for an egregious mistake could be understood as the analyst needs to be complied with. Every analyst tries to consider what the consequences of gratification might be but there is never certainty. An assessment of the narcis-sistic vulnerability of the analysand helps the analyst gage the degree of abstinence tolerable.

In principle, the need for abstinence makes good sense if not rigidly ascribed to. Early in the analysis if a question is asked, the analyst might say, "Why do you think you are asking me this question now?" or "I'm going to choose not to answer your question insofar as I feel this might deter us from learning more about why you are asking the question now." The analyst might add, "Once we are confident we understand why you are asking me the question, if you still wish to know the answer I will provide it." This is assuming the analyst believes that the answer will not burden the analysand.

My impression is that analysts first trained to work with children before training to treat adults, are less rigidly committed to abstinence. This is because working with children who have a lower *frustration tolerance*, has taught them that answering some questions or saying "Thank you" or " Hope your vacation goes well" does not derail an analysis. Nor does it prevent the expression of anger towards the analyst. The *real object relationship* affords children gratification. But adults are not children and more abstinence can be tolerated for the most part.

With some adult and adolescent analysands, the analyst must judge whether or not to limit food and drink in sessions, e.g., soda or coffee brought from outside. They may see it as interference. After several such instances, I prefer to wonder aloud about the meaning of the behavior and pose that to the analysand to ponder. I think an exception is with young children. I remember at the Hampstead Clinic the receptionist would provide cookies and milk in the waiting room to the children coming directly after school for their sessions. It is customary for parents to provide children with after school snacks, and children expect it. If a child brought a snack into a child analytic session I did not comment on it.

Setting a limit has to do with not violating the *boundaries* of either the analyst or analysand. By a boundary I mean the "personal space" of either so that the analyst will not feel his or her privacy has been violated, and the analysand will not feel pressured or encroached upon to reveal something before they are ready to do so. In contemporary times with the Internet the privacy of the analyst is often intruded upon by people either looking for a suitable professional to consult or by patients already in treatment who are curious about their analyst. Such intrusions do not irreparably impair transference development.

Some analysands prefer to be called by first name and to address me by my first name too. In a majority of instances this request came after a couple of years of analysis or after a former analysand returned for further treatment. It was suggested that after so many years of intimacy it felt it too formal to refer to me as "Dr. Sherick." I did not object and called them by first name too, putting aside the limit regarding acceptance of boundaries. The decision did not seem to cause unwanted results.

With young children, sometimes limits need to be made verbally and sometimes with physical restraint to stop destructive behavior towards the things in the consulting room play area, or towards the person of the analyst. The point is made maybe even in the first session, depending on the child's personal history, "In here you may say anything but you cannot do anything. You will not be allowed to hurt me, the things in the room, or yourself. I want you to feel safe." This is necessary because sometimes in an angry outburst a child may knock over a lamp or mark wallpaper with a crayon or even physically attack the analyst. With young children, too, they sometimes like to play "doctor" and want to examine the body of the analyst. I set limits, pointing out that a doll (I had a "Dr. Sherick" doll) represents me and I prefer it be examined rather than me. Rarely, did a child strongly object. Very young children may want to sit on the analyst"s lap. I think most child analysts would gently limit this, believing that it could get too exciting for the child. The feelings of safety for the child, and the analyst's own comfort level are the guiding principals in such limit setting. For each child there is an optimal distance for the child analyst to sit in proximity to the child. Some younger child analysts choose with young children who often play on the floor to sit alongside them on the floor.

Young children need to be told at some point that the play room needs to be left in the same way it was when they entered.

This is because children may wish to hang up on the wall a drawing they completed. The child analyst points out that what he or she and the child do during their time together is private, not to be shared with other children. That is why the child never sees drawings from other children in the room. This limit supports confidentiality and likely helps some children to feel special, a not uncommon childhood aspiration.

Earlier, in my comments about work with parents I spoke about conveying to them the confidentiality that will be abided by an analyst's in the work with their child, and the "limits" of confidentiality in work with them. The confidentiality of the child will not hold if the child's wellbeing is in doubt, e.g., if suicide is a strong possibility. If an analyst seriously is concerned about suicidal potentiality in an adolescent or adult, it is advisable to ask the analysand to "promise" to try to telephone the analyst if they are worried they may act on a suicidal thought. Of course, a promise is not binding, but most analysands respect the commitment.

As a non-physician I do not have requests made to me by analysands for medication of any kind, e.g., a sleeping pill, a tranquilizer, an anti-depressant, etc. There are psychoanalysts who are MDs and their analysands sometimes make such requests. I believe if these requests are complied with it complicates the relationship between the two. A limit should be made on such requests. In one instance they are acting as an analyst and in another as a physician. The analysand acts in one way towards their analyst and in another way towards their physician. It makes more sense to me to refer the analysand to a psychiatrist for a consultation if it is believed that analysis has gone "as far as it can" in alleviating *psychosomatic* symptoms.

Ways of Bringing Material

Analysts rarely have an agenda as to what should be the focus in a particular session. Suggestion is not a technique, nor is manipulation. Analysands decide the agenda in their own analysis. The understanding of a person's mind is based partly on the gradual peeling off of layers until you get to the core conflicts, much like peeling a piece of fruit. Occasionally, the analyst will introduce something at the beginning of a session, usually having to do with the frame, e.g., a schedule change, such as the analyst's vacation. It is introduced at the beginning in order to give the analysand time to react to the news. Sometimes an analysand has to miss a session or has some other bit of news and may delay mentioning this until they are ready to leave the hour. Presumably there is some meaning to this and a reluctance to deal with the associated feelings. If this happens regularly with a particular analysand the analyst will introduce it into a session.

With adults and adolescents, the major way material is brought into sessions is verbally. Occasionally, a photograph will be presented of someone or a pet that is often spoken about. With the advent of smart phones a text or email from someone will be read rather than reliance on memory. In contemporary time, some analysts have regular telephone or Skype sessions. I have not regularly had long-distance analytic sessions. I believe that there is a different quality in a session when analyst and analysand are present together. Occasionally, when reality intrudes I will have a telephone session, e.g., if a person is travelling a distance by car to get to a session and traffic is stalled because of an accident making it impossible for the analysand to arrive during the hour, we will talk on the phone. Some analysands will write down a dream in the middle of the night. While

I do not prohibit reading of notes, I point out what is in their mind is important and that forgotten details will return to memory once they try to associate to the dream.

It is not unusual for free association to be in the form of a metaphor that conveys a lot of meaning. For example, an adult male analysand said she "cut it off," referring to the verbal dispute he and his wife were having. After a moment he referred to his choice of words and commented about his castration fear of injury to his penis. What followed were childhood memories of similar worries.

Analysands of all ages have difficulty speaking about memories of traumatic experiences. It is very difficult for adults and adolescents to talk about trauma in sessions, and for young children to enact it in play. It is much too upsetting. They may feel dissociated whenever a memory of the trauma is "glimpsed" by the Ego. Analysts know that analysands cannot be "pushed" to talk about trauma; they must feel safe and allied with their analyst and feel hopeful that processing the traumatic events will be helpful to them. Talking about a past trauma allows for some *abreaction*, but while emotional discharge can be helpful, analytic processing of it, i.e., emotional understanding of it is more so. It is helpful when analysands begin to feel empowered and can confront their abusers.

Dreams and dream interpretation have had a significant history in psychoanalysis. Adults and adolescents, less so with younger children, may bring material in this manner. Dreams were once thought to be "the royal road" to the Unconscious (Ucs.). Nowadays we consider dreams as a road to the Ucs, but not the only road. A dream occurs during sleep when the *censor* between the unconscious and conscious part of the mind relaxes enough to allow repressed mental content access into the conscious part of the mind as long as it is disguised. Perhaps the sleep state makes it less likely that the repressed wishes will be expressed in action, and hence the censorship is not as strong. An experience of the day of the dream, the *day residue,* is seized by a repressed wish, perhaps because of a related meaning. A *latent dream* is constructed in the Ucs. Primitive primary processes of thinking, such as condensation, displacement, reversals, and substitution, form the latent dream. After more revision so as to be acceptable as a *manifest dream*, the Ego allows it to be recalled in a wakeful state. Freely associating to details in the dream and recognizing the meaning of the day residue, along with the current state of the transference and resistance, may allow the analytic couple to begin to understand the dream. Such processing of a dream often deepens the analysis.

Some analysands rarely bring dreams or say they dream but cannot remember them. Some may ask if it is helpful to record their memory of the dream after awakening or write down their memory. When this is asked there is likely a resistance to remembering and this is the primary focus. The analysand may admit preconceived notions about dreams based on movies or fiction and be afraid to reveal dreams. If a dream is reported early in an analysis it is helpful to give some education about the process of understanding the latent meaning from the manifest dream. It is important to impress upon the analysand that the meaning of a dream is dependent upon associations. The analyst is not a "mind reader." I think adult analysands appreciate knowing about this partnership, although, of course, some may use it to thwart the understanding of dreams. More analysis of resistance follows.

There are some common features of dreams. Reversals are often present, so that the representation of something in the present is really depicting something that happened in the past and vice versa. Dreams can employ phrases, words, and expressions or images that convey meaning. For example, an image of a "hail Mary pass " in a football game, might portray a wish for a miracle to change their life situation. Symbols are often used. Again, it is imperative to get associations to the symbol and not for the analyst to assume understanding of the meaning of the symbol, metaphor, or aphorism used by the analysand. Sometimes the symbol is meant to represent the dreamer's body or sexual intercourse.

A dream may have something to do with the analysand's feelings about the analytic process or about the analyst. For example, there may be a nurse in the dream who "thinks she knows everything, even more than the doctor." In this instance the nurse may be the analyst and the doctor the analysand. Sometimes there are multiple dreams in one night that the analysand reports. Such multiple dreams are usually related. The analyst is always alert to the possibility that an incident in the previous session is represented in the dream, lending continuity to the analysis.

There are "common dreams" such as punishment or rescue dreams. One common dream is an examination dream wherein the dreamer is failing an exam. The dreamer awakes and is reassured that he or she has not failed and has progressed in their life. There are some dreams that occur over and over separated by time in the dreamer's life. The repetition signifies some important event in their psyche.

A *daydream* is a daytime fantasy that a person deliberately playfully constructs, often to engage in a pleasurable, often reality denying, activity. An example is being capable of flying.

Often a symbol may convey important meanings. A older patient was fearing a decline of his mental and physical capacities. He had a dream that included the insect "slugs." Via associations we discovered the slugs represented both his fear of "slowing down" and his wish that his decline be slow. This understanding came only with my introducing the adjective "sluggish" into our analyzing the dream.

I have had a child who brought in a pet dog. A good part of the analysis centered around her behavior with the dog and/or my occasional displacement of interpretations to the dog when I thought doing so would allow her to hear my comment. Her behavior with the dog allowed her in a displaced way to express her feelings and thoughts about significant people in her life.

Younger children predominantly play. The material is in the story that is implicit in the play or explicitly narrated by the child alongside the play. The child is like the playwright or director of a play and the child analyst may be assigned a role. The child describes the analyst's part in the play. "You play a boy on the playground but be like a bully." "Be a strict teacher and I will be the smartest kid in the class." Sometimes children by themselves play out all the characters in their dramas.

Play is a mental activity like other mental activities and shares commonalities such as associated affects, defensive modifications, symbolism, etc. While it seeks gratification of the drive derivative being expressed, immediate gratification may not be sought.

Children also may elect to draw or use playdough, use a toy brought from home or use toys provided by the child analyst. For example, children build with blocks or Lego, use puppets, use toy soldiers, arrange miniature furniture in a dollhouse, and play with board games such as Snakes and Ladders, checkers or chess. The fundamental characteristic of play is *action*.

The analyst chooses toys based on the chronological age of the child. Toys are chosen that are capable of being creatively used in play, i.e., ones that do not have to adhere to rules, such as a board game. Sometimes, however, a board game serves a useful purpose for a child that is anxious. The rules allow the child to retreat from disclosing something at that moment which is making them anxious and could escalate. A child analyst will have a community of toys that all the children in his or her practice can use, while also having lockers or boxes in which toys selected for a particular child and those brought from home are used exclusively by the owner. Puppets, dolls of both genders, toy animals and soldiers, a doctor's examination kit, a doll house, etc., are examples of toys that can be selected. Baby dolls with appropriate genitalia of both genders allow young child opportunities to express thoughts about parental care and sexual identity. A child can use blocks at times when he or she needs to be uncommunicative, much like silence with an adult or adolescent. The analyst can address the silence of the adult or adolescent in an empathic manner, "You seem to wish to be within yourself today, judging from your silence." With a young child, I might say, "You are very quiet today. You seem to be building a wall behind which you hope to be safe, instead of playing."

Some child analysts believe play can be therapeutic even if no interpretations are made. Perhaps a distinction can be made between "therapeutic" and "analytic." The former can result from play because a discharge of feelings might take place and the child gets pleasure from the play. If a child has experienced a scary event, such as a medical procedure or a barking dog that jumped up on them, they may repeat the experience in their play. We call this turning a *passively* experienced event into an *actively* experienced event. The child often assigns the role of "victim" to the child analyst and he or she assumes the role of the perpetrator. Often, the child may not verbalize memory of the event, but the child analyst will have been told of its occurrence by the parents. The enactment of this passive experience into an active one probably has a therapeutic value. To have an analytic outcome, I would prefer to have play result in a partial resolution of a conflict, a diminution of anxiety, etc., which is more likely to be accomplished by the aid of interventions on the child analyst's part.

Adolescents also play. By the time adolescence is reached the cognitive abilities have matured from early concrete ways of thinking, to mature deductive reasoning, so that play moves, for the most part, from action to *playful thought.* Thought now becomes *trial action* wherein immediate gratification is less imperative, and fantasy is adopted as a major way to obtain satisfaction, at least partially. The child analyst working with an adolescent will follow the sequence of speech, much like free association. If there seems to be some resistance noticed using "close process analysis," this will be brought to the adolescent's attention. "Did you notice, your slip of the tongue?" or "Did you notice the long silence after you told me about your walking up the steps at school alongside a girl, you did not know, that you found to be very attractive?"

The child analyst with a young child observes the child's play, listens to his utterances or spoken words, tries to decipher the meaning of the play, may intervene to label a feeling being expressed by the child by attributing the affect to a character, deconstruct or decipher a symbol to get at the child's pre- or unconscious meaning. The analyst will watch to see if the play changes in ways that can be attributed to the impact upon the child by the interventions. If it does and the play is elaborated the deeper meaning might be inferred by the analyst. If the child seems ready in the child analyst's judgment to hear an interpretation about the meaning of the play, one may be offered and the child's reaction carefully noted.

Adolescents often talk about musical groups and songs that you have never heard. It seems to me that each generation of adolescents likes and has allegiance to music that is undecipherable to their parents' generation. I think it is one way that they seek independence. The child analyst expresses interest and asks to have the words spoken or sung or played on a smart phone and together with the adolescent seeks to understand the affinity of the analysand to the song. Analytic meaning can be learned in a fun way.

Comings and Goings

Arriving for an appointment and leaving at the end of an appointment essentially are part of the frame of the treatment, the essential aspects of which were introduced earlier. Prospective patients agreeing to enter psychoanalysis implicitly accept that they are expected to arrive punctually and leave when the time scheduled has expired. We know that the exigencies of life sometimes interfere with punctuality. Adult analysands usually offer an explanation for the cause of the lateness, e.g., an excessive unexpected amount of auto traffic. Adolescents are often late and may decry punctuality. When lateness becomes a characteristic of a particular adult or adolescent the analyst likely will conjecture that it has a meaning and will pose a comment to the analysand, "Have you noticed that you rarely come on time?" The hope is that the analysand will become curious, too, about whether there is a meaning to their lateness? Of course, the stronger the working alliance the more likely they will seriously consider that there may be a meaning. As a "rule of thumb" an analyst will not express that there may be a meaning about a particular manner of "coming" with one single instance, but wait to see if the analysand independently raises curiosity. Analysands differ as to whether or not they offer a greeting upon entering or being picked up in the waiting room. Some simply say "Hello", while some might say "How are you?" We presume there may be a meaning beyond social convention but likely not to be understood until later in the analysis or until the analysand raises it or has a free association to it.

With children "comings" are more complicated. After all, their parents bring them usually, so punctuality or tardiness may not be due to them, unless you learn that the child delayed meeting the parents at a designated place for the departure to a session. Some children greet the child analyst with a hug, others run ahead into the consulting room, while others eagerly accompany the analyst. If the location of the office lends itself to it, a child might play "hide-and-seek" and exclaim with joy or regret when you "find" him. Again, the meaning of the beginning of a session for a particular child may have to wait awhile until the child's *dynamics* are better understood. But at the first few episodes the child analyst might say, " You seem to want me to either find you or not find you at the beginnings of our time together. I wonder why?" As with older analysands, the intervention is aimed at arousing the child's curiosity about their behavior (mind).

Departures at the end of a session also likely have meanings that will take time to understand. Some adults say, "Thank you," others simply say "Goodbye," or simply leave without consistently saying anything. In some cultures, an adult may shake your hand on coming and going because this is the polite thing that adults do with one another. Young children may join you in the request to clean up the room, i.e., put toys away, in compliance with the limit set at the beginning of the analysis. "We will try to keep the play area looking at the end of a session as it looked at the beginning." Most children comply although there are some who do not because of their particular dynamics, e.g., *anal expulsive* issues. Some children wish to hang up a drawing of theirs in non-compliance with the request that the room be the way it was when they started the session. Often this is motivated by exhibitionistic or competitive feelings regarding other children seen by the child analyst. For some children, the request to bring something home from the session is an expression of a preconscious wish to extend their time with the analyst, a wish that the analyst can make conscious if there is confidence in its meaning.

Role of Education

The early history of psychoanalysis involved a debate about making the patient as "free" as possible to talk about the thoughts on this or her mind. Thus any intervention or instruction by the analyst that involved suggestion was frowned upon. Free association became the ideal way for analysands to bring psychic material with the analyst maintaining a position of *neutrality.* Classically, what this meant was that the analyst would not favor the Id, Superego, or Ego in listening or in interpreting. The analyst was to listen in a non-biased manner "equidistant" from the instinctual desires (Id), the moral commitments (Superego), and the reality concerns (Ego) of the analysand. Imposing values onto the analysand was unacceptable, although we now appreciate that countertransference is ubiquitous so that the analyst's values do influence, to some degree, how things are heard and responded to by the analyst.

Educating the analysand was held to have no or very little place in psychoanalysis as a technique. Essentially it was thought that a consequence could be an imposition of a viewpoint upon the analysand and in some way compromising the neutrality of the analyst. While I accept this, I think there are times in an analysis with analysands of all ages, especially children, where education has a beneficial value. With an adult, at the beginning of an analysis when the analyst explains the "basic rule" of free association and answers questions as to why the couch is recommended, an educational intervention is being made. Some analysts choose to refrain from giving the "basic rule" or suggesting the value of a supine position on the analytic couch. They prefer to let the analysand proceed as they choose, addressing resistance to speaking freely and use of the couch on the occasion when the analysand notes curiosity of its presence.

A quasi-educational intervention with adults and adolescents that I often use when early origin of conflicts is noted by the analysand, is to point out that we all have a child within us, so to speak, and that we can help the child grow up to be an adult or adolescent, using the resources we now have that the child did not have. Sometimes, I have found it useful to point out the universality of a conflict, such as the Oedipus Complex, or that of the mind that seeks pleasure and avoids "unpleasure," to help them emotionally understand "resistance." This educational imparting of a bit of psychoanalytic clinical theory, used judiciously, I have found to have beneficial value.

Earlier, I referred to interpretive interventions that deal with reactive depression and normal guilt. I made the point about how it is important with some analysands to "normalize" both these feeling states. While such interventions are interpretive they also contain an educative component, namely, distinguishing "normal" from "pathological."

I find it helpful to point out the potential value for analysands who have been "abused" to confront their abuser. They need to be prepared that an apology may not be forthcoming but that they still might feel better regarding their sense of self-agency. Another "educative" intervention is to point out the value of "self-forgiveness" after feeling remorse and making amends about a transgression.

Distinguishing between anger and assertion can be extremely important for some adult and adolescent analysands. It often is an intervention that is educational as part of interpretive work focusing on the use of *passivity* as a defense against anger. The analysand is afraid that if they set limits or are critical of a spouse, e.g., that they will be destructive. It is as if they feel such an expression will get out of control. After processing the anger, it can be helpful to distinguish the difference between anger and assertiveness. I think this is an educational intervention. The self-empowering feeling that can follow when one sets limits on someone who has exceeded the limits of civility gives an analysand a sense of hopefulness that they can protect themselves in an adult manner.

With young children, it is natural for them to look to an adult to guide them and to help them understand novel situations. This being so, the child analyst is helping them to feel safe both with their inner worlds as well as the outer world. This lends itself to occasional comments about how some of the child's actions cause him or her to feel unsafe, either because of worry the "inner policeman" (the superego) or mommy, daddy, teacher, etc., will disapprove. There are other times when the child analyst needs to impart or correct misunderstandings about, e.g., how babies are made, the different external and internal anatomy of males and females, what "divorce" means, etc. Of course, education is not given without first hearing the child's own understanding of the issue. What one is providing is a correction to clear up confusion. Earlier, I referred to a child analyst being a "real" and or "developmental" object to a child analysand. With young child I would use a plastic doll that had internal organs that could be seen. I also had baby dolls of each gender with the appropriate genitalia. Ideally, sexual education is best learned in the context of a parent-child relationship, but, regretfully, this is often not the case because of the absence or inability of a parent to do so.

Work with Parents

It used to be that child analysts did not believe that it was essential to see parents conjointly when one was seeing their child or adolescent in psychoanalysis. This attitude has changed drastically in the past thirty years. We once thought that we only needed to get the parents to support their child's treatment, to pay the fees and to transport the child to his or her sessions.

Partly, this was based on the model of adult analysis where the analysand is the sole person in treatment and the analysis proceeded on the basis only of what transpired in the consulting room. Another issue was the lack of confidence of child analysts that they were truly practicing psychoanalysis and not play therapy as some of their only-adult trained colleagues were contending. Hence, they treated child and adolescent patients as mini-adults. With adolescents there existed the observations that a developmental need of that age group was to achieve independence from parents. To support this developmental need child analysts did not include parents in the process.

With preoediplal children, sometimes they cannot separate from their mothers. She will have to be in the consulting room for a period of time until the child can feel safe alone with the child analyst. This could be a matter of a number of sessions or even weeks. Sometimes, the child refuses to leave the lap of the mother. With time, however, the child will allow the mother to leave. The mother or the child analyst may initiate this permission from the child.

We now know better. We recognize that there is no child without parents. Also, we realize that child analysts need to build a working alliance with parents as well. We do this for more reasons than they pay our fees. We know that a child or adolescent in analysis will reach a point when there is a wish to quit and it is the parents' support of the treatment that keeps the child or adolescent in the analysis. With adolescents, while we support them in their wish to become more independent from their parents we do not believe that severing ties with parents is in the best interests of most adolescents. Rather, except in some cases of abusive parents, we try to help the adolescent and his or her parents revive the healthier and growth promoting aspects of their former relationship. We state this openly to both parties.

With adolescent patients and some older preadolescents when we see their parents we offer them the opportunity to attend the parent sessions. Most opt not to attend. I do not believe this choice is a sign of psychopathology but rather an intuitive recognition of the need for privacy. Child analysts are not in favor of keeping secrets but are in support of privacy.

Initial work with parents is to help them understand that their child's "problems" are not because of disobedience or personal choice but because of neurotic conflict. Once they appreciate this then they are much more allied with the child analyst. Sometimes, a child analysis may have to be delayed until the parents can accept this formulation. It is essential, too, that parental self-blame for their child's issues and aspiration to be "good" parents not be over-looked in the initial contacts. "Strengths" need to be focused on along with "weakness" in parenting.

My understanding is that working with parents is not the same as viewing them as patients. It is more focused on issues of parenting. I believe that if the parent work becomes psychotherapy with the parent couple or with one of the parents, issues can arise that will undermine the analysis with their child. One parent may develop transference to the child analyst and become competitive with his or her child as they once did with a sibling. Of course, this can happen in parent work too, but it is less likely if the kind of controlled regression in a treatment is not encouraged.

Analysts are now very aware of the *intergenerational transmission of psychopathology.* Hence, in parent work we want to get a picture of the parents' respective childhoods and their relationship with their own parents. Doing so we can help parents understand if they have identified with their own parents' style of parenting, or if they have identified their child with one of their own siblings and have a transference to them based on their past dealings with a sibling.

Parents can appreciate that the child analyst's work with their child is confidential, except if it is necessary for them to be notified that their child, usually an adolescent, is seriously considering suicide. First, the adolescent would be encouraged to share this with their parents before the analyst tells them this. The child analyst also tells parents that what they talk about will not be treated confidentially. The child analyst will, at his or her discretion, tell the child or adolescent what the parents have shared with him or her if it is believed to be in the best interests of the analysand to be told. Parents are encouraged in such instances to share with their child what they have told the analyst at an opportune time. Of course, there are some parents who have trouble not knowing details about what transpires in their child's treatment. When this is noticed, work with a parent such as this deals with the psychic dynamics of his or her "need to know."

What does the child analyst do with extra-analytic material obtained, e.g., from a teacher? Presumably, the analyst has obtained permission from the parent to talk to the teacher, and from an older child as well. I think each analyst will use judgment about what, how, and when to share the information with the child.

With very young children, their belief in the *omnipotence* of their parents, appears to run counter to efforts to assure them of confidentiality; after all, their parents "know" everything. Nevertheless, there will be occasions when this belief will be weakened and confidentiality will emerge as a concern.

When working with parents, as with analysands, a child analyst needs to be aware of countertransference. Sometimes, a child analyst may feel they could do a better job parenting than the child or adolescent's parents can accomplish. He or she may become competitive with the parents.

Parent work with mothers and their infants or toddlers is a specialization of some child analysts. Fathers can also benefit. We know that parenting is a difficult endeavor. Parents can provide nurturance but also they can burden a very young child with their own psychopathology. Above, I have pointed out intergenerational transmission of psychopathology. Hence, a mother might react towards an infant or toddler son that has an outburst of angry feelings as if he was her father. Here a mother is putting aside, unconsciously, her *objective reality* and responding to her *psychic reality* wherein there is an equation between her son and her father. With an infant, an analyst might intervene with an anxious mother by offering interpretations about how hard it seems to feel her infant is separate from herself, insofar as the infant was once inside of her. A mother coming out of a postpartum depressive episode can be reassured that the guilt she is feeling for having neglected her infant is not pathological and underscores her devotion to her baby. It can be pointed out that her comforting ministrations hereon will go a long way to helping her infant develop normally.

Sometimes, educative interventions are helpful. An analyst might help a parent to distinguish between different types of outbursts from their young child, e.g., anxiety or fear, from frustration. A parent can benefit from knowing the likely developmental trajectory soon to unfold based on their child's chronological age. A father can be helped to deal with his envy when his spouse seems overly attentive to her nursing infant and he feels ignored.

Goals of Psychoanalytic Treatment

Psychoanalysis does not claim to "cure" people of mental distress. Nor does it claim to "eradicate" mental conflict. Mental conflict is universal and ubiquitous. A psychoanalytic treatment is successful if it makes an analysand more aware of his or her conflicts, so that the conscious mind can allow into awareness what was once forbidden. With greater tolerance for anxiety a less neurotic solution than one formerly used can be achieved. Insofar as the reaction time is reduced when the person becomes aware of the conflict, a more rational, adaptive solution can be affected than the usual neurotic one. Analysts focus less on goals and more on the process of analysis.

The initial goals of analyst and analysand often do not correspond with one another. Patients enter analysis often with life goals that have been elusive, e.g., to find a compatible life partner. All patients wish to be relieved of symptoms, e.g., an eating pickiness. Also, they seek to be happier in their life, less depressed and cynical. An adolescent or younger child may want to be more popular, less shy around peers.

While analysts would hope that these goals would be achieved during psychoanalysis, they focus less on life goals, symptom relief, and social success, and more on *intrapsychic* changes. That is, modification in the way the mind manages conflict. An analytic aim would be a Superego that is more mature and relativistic in its moral compass, a Self that is more secure in it's self-esteem, not needing external "applause" to feel valued, an Ego that in its judgment recognizes that a deed is different from a thought or fantasy, an Ego that is more tolerant of the desires and feelings of all kind so that defensive maneuvers are not immediately necessary. Insofar as desires and needs are not always gratified, the heightening of frustration tolerance is a goal of psychoanalytic treatment. Also, greater tolerance for anxiety is also a goal of analysis. It is hoped that the analysand has examined core conflicts and that neurotic solutions are not sought but rather more adaptive ones. *Sublimation* of the aims of the expression of instinctual drives is also welcomed. We mean that more socially acceptable aims replace ones less so. For example, for a child, anal-explosive impulses to mess are replaced by a wish to paint colors on an easel. With an adolescent, a wish to hurt a rival by drawing blood is replaced by a passion to become an expert fencer, and later to become a surgeon. At the end of an analysis it is hoped that the analysand has identified with the analyzing function of the analyst and will carry on with self-analysis after the treatment ends.

An analyst endeavors to educate an analysand that personal conflicts are not eradicated by psychoanalysis, that mental conflict is ubiquitous and universal. Most analysands can accept this, including young children. A child can be told that there will be times when he or she will feel scared (anxious), and that is alright because he or she now knows that the "inner policeman" will not seek punishment for only a "naughty" thought.

With adolescents an aim of the analyst is to help them and their parents resume a healthier relationship wherein the former feels supported by the parents, while also feeling more independent from them. Most adolescents welcome this as an outcome. They understand that severing ties with parents is not sensible except if the parents are abusive and unwilling to change.

With younger children, the analyst aims to return the childs' development on a progressive trajectory. You will recall the discussion above about fixation points, which cause development to halt, sometimes in a partial way but sometimes in a major way. The child analysis hopefully undoes the fixation by an emotional understanding and *catharsis*. Having an analysis as a child does not prevent later neurotic issues but it can help the older child deal with it more effectively.

In psychoanalytic developmental theory, reaching the Oedipal phase and dealing with it is believed to be a beneficial experience for an individual. Hence, a goal of work with children dealing predominantly with *preoedipal* issues is to resume progressive development and hope that they will struggle with the Oedipal Complex. Regretfully, in some instances a two-parent household may be non-existent. While this makes it more difficult for the child to deal with Oedipal issues it does not make it impossible. Kids are resourceful and a relative, teacher, or community leader can be employed in their psyche to play the role of the absent parent.

The internalization of parental authority in the form of the Superego, results in an internal "inner policeman," albeit a "harsh" one to begin with. Over time the Superego becomes more mature. The struggle with the Oedipal Complex often results in a de-idealization of the parents and eventually a more realistic image of them as people with faults but also redeeming characteristics. The internalization of a Superego and the partial dissolution of the Oedipal Complex allows for Latency to begin. We call this *infantile amnesia*. Now less burdened by strong *instinctual wishes*, the child can begin to deal with and learn coping skills to adapt to the external world. It is no wonder that formal education begins the advent of Latency. The strengthening of the Ego vis-à-vis the Id will allow the child to be prepared with a better defensive armamentarium to deal with the advent of puberty and the re-strengthening of the sexual and aggressive drives. Child analysis has as an aim the strengthening of the child's ego.

With older adults, dealing with *existential issues* is very beneficial. They are ubiquitous but not everyone grapples with them. Hopefully in an analysis, the analyst, who also has such issues, has been able to help the analysand deal with them.

Working Through

Every analyst has had the experience of having an analysand, usually adult but also adolescent, react with an "Ah,ha" sense of relief about a breakthrough insight after the analyst has made an interpretation. The analyst will be pleased but also note, privately, that the same interpretation has been made countless times before without the profound sense by the analysand that they have had a major insight. What accounts for the change? Perhaps one should not look a "gift horse in the mouth." I think it is helpful for an analyst to comment on "progress" that the analysand is showing, commenting on the analysand's own words until now that they "seem unable to get out from under" a particular self-defeating behavior. Such comments strengthen the working alliance. When there are frequent "ah, ha!" type expressions by the analysand, termination may be forthcoming in the near future.

We call the above phenomenon *working through*. It underscores the persistence of neurotic solutions to mental conflicts. What has reduced anxiety in the past for the neurotic individual is accepted as a valuable tool even if it is self-defeating. The resistance or dynamic process has to be interpreted many times before the insight is convincing. It is as if what is required is the cumulative effect of multiple insights to weaken the resistance of the unconscious ego, and effect a structural change, i.e., an effect that is not time-limited. There seems to be a tendency on the part of the mind, most likely a characteristic of the Id to engage in a *repetition compulsion*. This characteristic could be considered an Id resistance. This type of resistance is also encountered with the Ego regarding character defenses. As mentioned earlier, these are defenses that have proven their neurotic usefulness countless times so they become like a personality signature.

An adult analysand after four years of analysis, had a stomach ache and worried that he might have an accident and soil. A memory occurred of a childhood soiling incident wherein he felt ashamed. Father took him home from school to clean him up and did not shame him. The analysand had just concluded a successful business venture and was feeling adult and masculine. I commented that in the Ucs money and feces are equated. He immediately responded with memories of "dirty money" from his childhood. This money was obtained by relatives from exploited customers and not reported as income. I said he has transformed soiling to spending money on commercial ventures that benefitted himself and the community, giving him a sense of pride and accomplishment, different from the shame he felt as a child, adolescent, and young adult when he felt he disappointed his father. Additionally, I said this was a sign of progress. Working through displays progressive steps of progress. Defenses are loosened, even given up, and feelings of self-actualization occur.

Termination

Analysands often wish to know during a treatment, how will they know or how will the analyst know when it is time to end. This topic was considered earlier when we discussed the aims or goals of analysis from the analysand and analyst perspectives. This is a legitimate question with no easy answer. Putting aside the unilateral ending of an analysis because the adult moves to another state, or the adolescent goes off to an out-of-state college, or the family of the young adult or child analysand incurs unexpected debts and the cost of analysis is prohibitive. Of course, regarding the latter, the fee can be reduced permanently or temporarily. Nowadays, if an analysand moves away, some analysts via telephone or via Skype practice long distance analysis, with occasional in-person visits by the analysand. Sometimes, the best-made plans cannot be achieved.

In some respects an analysis does not ever end, insofar as one of the aims of the analyst is that after termination the analysand will continue to identify with the analyzing function of the analyst and engage in self-analysis.

Eradicating all mental conflict cannot be the criterion insofar as eradication is not possible. With adults we aim before stopping to have analyzed to some degree the entire major conflicts that have been identified during the analysis. The key word here is "major" insofar as minor ones may not have been able to "compete" with major ones for attention. Again, here is where we hope the analysand will feel confident that he or she can do some self-analysis.

When the analyst is thinking of termination, a consideration is the quality of the transference. Once the adult analysand is reacting towards the analyst as another adult and not as a special kind of adult like a parent, then he or she is feeling less regressed and "the child within the adult' analysand has "grown up." A major aim of the analysis has likely been achieved.

With young children and adolescents, termination is considered once progressive movement in development has been reinstated. This presumably will be possible, as with adults, once the core conflicts have been sufficiently analyzed. The same criterion is a determinant in the decision to stop analysis with some young adults who are essentially prolonging their adolescence. If we think of adult stages of development, we can also think of progressive development being restarted, e.g., if an adult who was once afraid of becoming a parent now can consider that status, or even look forward to it.

Once the analyst and analysand agree to terminate, a termination date is set, and the termination stage begins. The termination period varies in length depending on individual cases, but I would say the average length of time is at least three to six months. Some analysts ask the analysand to assume a sitting position facing the analyst. Some analysands request this too. It is done because the transference has been more-or-less resolved and two adults of "equal" status can now talk "face to face." Some analysts also reduce the frequency of sessions from four or five to two or three. It is to discourage regression. I believe, however, that the frequency and the use of the couch should be maintained until the last day, except if the analysand wishes a change. My thought is that there are termination issues that best be talked about and the maintaining of the frame best encourages this to happen.

The major issue that needs to be talked about is the analysand's feelings about the ending. Are they sad because of the ending? Does it remind them of significant losses from the past, e.g., the death of a grandparent or the relocation of a friend to a distant city, or moving from elementary school to middle school, etc.

With many young children and adolescents, they will express pleasure that with the ending of the analysis they will again have more free time after school. With some of these analysands, the analyst may elect to continue with their parents. The feelings of these children about that prospect need to be considered.

There may be some voiced expression of whether the analyst will agree to be seen again after the ending on an as-needed basis. Often this request is not followed up on, but analysts may hear from a former child patient when they have become older, sometimes with a request to resume analysis. Almost no analyst will contact a former patient for a follow-up to see how he or she is doing. It is believed that this would be an intrusion.

Termination is a " leave taking," of sorts. It is likely reminiscent in the Unconscious of other "leave takings" in development. I'm thinking of the toddler who beginning to walk toddles away from the arms of its caregiver or the sight of this person. I presume the toddler, when he falls, at some level, regrets leaving the arms and sight of the *omnipotent* adult. The oedipal child who de-idealizes his parents and internalizes them as structures in his mind, I presume feels a loss of the "perfect" parent, and may regret this "leave taking." The adolescent during the *second-individuation* phase must feel lonely or bereft to some degree that the bond with protective parents is weakened, another "leave taking." All of these prior experiences likely re-trigger the feelings of leave-taking connected to termination. During this phase the analyst and analysand will have occasion to connect contemporary feelings with earlier ones, and this will help in the processing of feelings of loss. This process may facilitate identification with the analyst's analyzing function akin to the oedipal-latency child's identification with the rule-giving parent of the same gender at the time of the partial dissolution of the Oedipal Complex.

At the termination of an analysis the expectation is that the transference will have been more-or-less resolved. One sign of this, mentioned above, is that the analysand acts and feels as if he or she is the equal to the analyst. The adult analysand will no longer feel like a child or adolescent vis-a-vis the adult analyst.

Some children may choose not to contact their former analyst later in life, even if they need more analysis, the reason being that the former analyst in their memory is in the context of "childhood" which they wish to leave behind. Adults may contact their former analyst when life's circumstances make them feel a brief return would be helpful. In my experience this is not uncommon. They may or may not choose to use the couch.

Part Three

Brief Clinical Illustrations

Below are illustrations of the clinical process of Psychoanalysis with two children, an adolescent, and two adults, followed by work with parents. Regretfully, a complete account of the analyses is not possible in the context of the aims of my book. I will give illustrations of the beginning of our work, the middle, and the end. First sessions can be very meaningful. It is as if a first session gives as preview of what is to follow. I have made the necessary biographical changes to insure confidentiality and anonymity.

Case #1)

A 4 ½ year old boy separated from his mother without apparent difficulty the first session and the rest of the week. He was referred because of anxiety and eating difficulties. He asked me what I would like to do. When I returned the question back to him he said, "It's your room." Thus, he took charge. He told me he was "strong" when it came time to remove the lids from the jars of playdoh. Towards the end of the hour he pretended he was a doctor and cared for my injured finger. Earlier he had told me of injuring his finger in the car door and was wearing a band-aid. Just before telling me of his injury, he told me how he and his father had "horrible fights at night." He lined up all the animals so that all but the last one, the "smallest" one, a lamb, had its tail bitten by the animal next in line. Then the soldiers shot the animals and each other. The animals then gathered around a fallen soldier and consumed him. He whispered the parts of the body being eaten (the analysand only ate meat contained in Heinz baby food). The material at the beginning of this analysis strongly suggested a boy dealing with phase adequate castration anxiety colored by an oral fixation.

Approximately six months later, he was disappointed because I saw what was in the bag he had brought. He complained about having no "surprise" until his mother reminded him of something in the bag. On the way to the room he had me guess what the surprise was. It was a "spy face" - by means of a magnet one could move metal shavings into different positions to make an indeterminate number of faces. He discovered it needed cellophane tape on it and went into the waiting room to ask his mother to fix it. I pointed out how his mother was the "fixer" like I was the previous session. We then played with cars he also had brought in. We enacted a television show that had to do with a car crash. The police wanted to shoot the guilty person and he asked me to decide if they should. I said it was a frightening thought to him that a naughty person should be shot but part of him thought it was a just penalty. He decided to shoot the man. After some more crashes I was a nighttime robber and the police (the analysand) chased me on a dangerous highway. He ran over a ghost but it was all right because he was the President. After awhile, I said he tells me about the nighttime and how exciting and frightening it can be. I pointed out how nighttime is a frightening time for many children because of the sounds they hear and other things they imagine and because it is dark and their parents are in another room. He said it isn't frightening in a car and told me how a friend's grandmother saw a lion from her car in Africa and she wasn't frightened. At the end of the hour he didn't want to tidy up or carry anything into the waiting room. I commented about the big boy-little boy conflict within him- he then helped. He wanted us to use different routes to the waiting room and I commented about separation and reunion and connected this to separation feelings during a recent holiday separation from me.

After three years of analysis termination affirmatively was decided upon. Progressive development had resumed. Our ending revived death wishes and guilt feelings connected with separations from his parents when they went on a vacation, as well as rivalrous Oedipal feelings with father (I learned from mother that her husband was traveling outside the country on business.) He requested to play chess. I reminded him how in a recent session he pretended to be an older brother to a younger one (me). They played after school, and did no home work. I spoke of his impatience to learn the skills of older children like his brother who seems so far ahead that he feels he'll never catch up. He switched the material to Oedipal rivalry. He pretended to be like father, an expert chess player, playing chess blindfolded and winning over three men (me) who joined together as a team. He wanted me to let him win so he could duplicate father's feat.

He was late for his final week of sessions. I learned father was home again from his business trip. I commented about his scary dream the previous week as "haunting" him because of his inner policeman and loving feelings in conflict with angry ones directed at father. He told me to "fuck off" and to stop speaking. At the end of the session he told me he would leave the Lego house we built earlier in the session intact for a "long time." I told him I recognize he has good feelings too. The next day we played a board game that I won but he pretended that he won. I was a silly younger brother. Within my role I spoke about my envy and the hardship of being the youngest member of the family. As a treat I got to go to school with my older brother. Fighting broke out between the older and younger boys. I spoke about my fear that if I did well an older boy would hurt me. I was told to "Shut up."

At our next to last session, he repeatedly said "I'm sorry to say…" He did not finish the sentence. I told him there was a song that goes "I'm sorry to say I'm on my way, won't be back for many a day…" He then killed an insect. I said he felt safer killing it than me or his parents and brother. He smiled and called me a "fart." At our last session he was teary but stoic. I shook his hand and said "Goodbye." Near tears he said, "I'll never forget you," and I said I would never forget him. Given an opportunity to take a toy home from his private drawer he chose a pistol. He said he could not find his pistols at home but if he found another he could play cowboys and Indians with a friend. We walked to the waiting room together. Before we ended I met with mother. I learned that she thought her son was much less anxious and less restricted in his appetite for foods.

Case # 2)

In our first analytic session, a nine-year-old girl who brought in a drawing, sat down on the opposite side of a play table. She was referred because of separation issues. She looked about the room. For the first three quarters of this session she was not spontaneous; I broke periods of silence. Throughout she smiled, a bit forced, and did not seem to be too uncomfortable. I asked about her drawing. It was of a squirrel walking across a fallen tree. The sky was very blue with a bright sun and the grass was very green. She likes to draw but most of the time in school is spent on arithmetic and reading. I wondered, after a silence, if she was wondering what sort of person I would turn out to be? She decided to draw another picture like the one she brought in but was dissatisfied with the outcome. We talked a bit about her unhappiness that an older brother was moving on to a different school than the one they were both attending. I explained the schedule I was going to propose to her parents later in the week. After another silence I asked if she likes to draw animals. She commented she liked "all" animals. I said I thought she brought a drawing of an animal to our first meeting to show me her fondness for animals. From here on she was more spontaneous about her interest in animals and her affect seemed more real. At the end of the session mother had come to pick her up and brought along her pet dog. I petted the dog. I felt at the end of the session that she looked forward to return.

Approximately six months later, she ran to the play room on her first day back following her school break and family vacation. She was silent, smiled, stuck her tongue out, and twirled the key to her toy drawer while humming "around the world in eighty days." Later she opened the window but closed it because she asked and learned I preferred it open. I commented she was angry with me. Later she asked if I took my dog on vacation with me and if I did not I would be cruel. I said she may feel I was cruel for not taking her and it may have seemed as if I was around the other side of the world. I related this to similar feelings as a younger girl when her parents were away on vacation or out for the evening. She rejected this; her family is "one big happy family." Then she told me it was her mother's anniversary but she would not say more because I do not tell her about my marriage. I spoke to how excluded she felt from a part of my life as she does from her parents' life. We then played a school game, with her as the teacher, for the remainder of the session. I said she copes with feelings of loss by wishing to control things.

In a meeting with her parents, they expressed pleasure with the changes over the past three years. Their daughter was more mature emotionally, coped better, did not panic when anxious, and no longer had stomach aches. In the sessions in the next to last week she played a bossy controlling teacher and I was a young child. Via this game she reversed roles and defended against feelings of helplessness connected with our ending. In my role as the child, I verbalized how I was being scolded because of my "naughtiness." She said I was an old man. I said she felt childish sometimes and thought I was too old to like. She smiled and wished me a horrible weekend. Underneath her façade of insults I sensed her fondness and love for me and I pointed out how it was difficult for her to express the good feelings openly. In our last session her tears were expressed in displacement. Her teacher cried at a meeting with parents and students. The teacher was moving away. My analysand expressed gratitude towards the teacher and bought her a gift. She worked on a watercolor painting and left the water faucet on for most of the session (symbolic crying?) and wet the picture till it was "sopping." She expressed curiosity about other children I see while she picked plaster off the wall. After setting a limit I expressed how she felt excluded and perhaps she thought we were ending because she does naughty things with her hands. She called me "stupid" and left the room but returned. She wanted to know what I would do with the contents of her private drawer. She refused my offer to take something home. She smiled and said she might send me a photo of her mare and foal (a recent family acquisition) and then left.

Case #3)

In the first session with a 13 ½ year old boy, he could not think of anything to say. He had been referred because of feeling "the odd man out at school." His father had unexpectedly died about a year earlier. I said that people find it helpful to say whatever comes into their minds. "Mathematics?" He said he always thinks of mathematics but did not wish to speak about it. I suggested he should not select what to speak about. He complained about all the television shows he would miss because of appointments. He again complained of nothing to say. I said perhaps he does not know where to begin and suggested he begin anywhere. He grimaced and looked about the room. I said it was natural for him to feel a bit uncomfortable and not sure about what to speak about since I was a stranger. I recalled to myself that the first time we met he was reading a book titled "In the Silence of the Night." I wondered if he was anticipating silences. He corrected me; it was "The City and the Stars." "Everyone gets things wrong, especially my mother. You say one thing and people say another thing." I said, "And now I got something wrong." He said he was tired and remained silent and uneasy. I said silence was fatiguing to him. A little later I wondered aloud if I recalled the title incorrectly because a part of me was responding to what he said the first time we met, namely that he found speaking difficult. I may have been anticipating that silence would make him feel uncomfortable. He was relieved when our time was up and said as he left, "Not an eventful day."

Approximately six months later, he was very late for a Monday appointment. He asked what time he arrived and said "Ugh" when told. He said I looked annoyed. Later a lot of birds flew over-head and he wondered why such a group is not called a "crowd" as with humans. The next day he was late again, although not so late as the prior session. When I queried him about the reasons for his lateness I learned he waits for his brother. He doesn't like to walk to the bus stop alone as it is getting dark because he passes a church that has a large crucifix in the front. He is afraid the figure will come alive, although he knows this cannot actually happen. He felt his fear was because he has not fully accepted the finality of his father's death. In death the body is "inert" but the brain and mind are still operating. If the latter could contact the former the person would be alive again.

There was a silence and a comment about a "sunrise." I said I thought he was hoping his father could reappear. He confirmed this notion. I said perhaps he also thought that some telepathic communication was possible. He said he never thought of this between a dead and living person but has thought it could happen between two living people. Later he noticed that some furniture in the consulting room had been moved. I said he was "observant." He responded he feels uncomfortable otherwise. He could not sleep in a room he does not know about; he opens up drawers, looks in cupboards, and locks drawers. What was he expecting to find? "What we were speaking about before," but he did not want to go further with this. He expects the usual contents to be in a cupboard but...I said only a part of him expects to discover something unusual. Later he imaged a woman in high heels sitting in the tree outside in the garden; he imagined this from the formation of the branches. I linked such imagined content to the idea that his father might reappear. He replied he could imagine anything. I said he has control over his mind and does not permit some images to emerge. I said the hope but fear that his father would reappear may put him off. He agreed.

After approximately two years of analysis we had a forced termination because my analysand and his mother moved to another state. After dealing with his resistance he was able to express some anger about our ending. He invited me to a concert and I accepted insofar as we were ending and I believed it would be a narcissistic injury to refuse. He did not see me at the concert and had doubts that I attended. He then talked about a movie he had seen where US cavalry slaughter native-Americans. He was surprised about having enjoyed the film, along with depressive feelings. He felt guilty. He accepted he had sadistic thoughts like other people. My attempts to connect such thoughts with doubts that I attended the concert did not evoke a reply from him. The week before we planned to end, he told me about a party he went to the night before and danced in group dances and enjoyed himself. It was nearing the end of the school year and some of his classmates would not be returning the next semester. I said August was a difficult month for him. He agreed and said his father "left' in August too. There's a book titled "August Was a Difficult Month" which he doesn't intend to read. I suggested after he gets settled in his new residence he contact a colleague and arrange a meeting. (We had both agreed he was not ready to end.) He said, "Not right away." When he finished a book he does not want to start another immediately. It would be "disrespectful" to do so. I said I appreciated his feeling and reminded him of his loyalty conflicts about father and me, and that both of us, I was sure, would not think him disloyal if he formed a relationship with another person. I said maybe he will feel different in a few months. We shook hands. He put his head on his hands resting on his elbows resting on his knees. As we left I told him my colleague liked music (a passion of his). He smiled and said that would help. He did meet a few times with my colleague but ended unilaterally soon thereafter.

Case# 4)

The analysand was a self-referred 32year old Caucasian female graduate student in Social Work. She referred herself because of anxiety that she attributed to the competitiveness of her graduate program. She also reported feeling "regressed" in terms of self-feelings, feeling depressed and "deviant." She was accepted for a low-fee analysis.

In our very first session, her fantasy of expecting to be abandoned was manifested. She came a couple of hours early for her first session, having gotten the appointment time confused. Her confusion seemed to indicate turning a passive expectation into an active possibility. Later, before assuming a reclining position on the couch, she indicated that her boots had mud on them and wondered if she should take them off. In a session during her first week she reported a dream where she was in a garment bag, and later associated to a garbage bag. Her feeling was that I would reject her and throw her out. She was a potentially attractive looking woman, but her appearance had a peculiar quality about it, a "second-hand Rose" touch. She gave off an impression of having "street sense." She had an older brother and sister. Father required hospitalization for a paranoid state and committed suicide when she was in her mid-twenties.

Resistance was initially manifested in the form that she had to be refined and have no feelings. Early in the treatment she was taken by surprise about feelings that seemed to be emerging about me. It was no coincidence that a relationship with a young man started to intensify as she entered analysis, and this was pointed out to her. A major resistance was externalization. A fear was that I would diagnose her as hysterical with an interest in older men. A fear of going crazy was also underneath her initial resistance. The initial transference was an expectation that she would feel violated by an interpretation. (Much later I learned that a former male therapist alluded to sexual feelings for her.) My precise verbalizations reminded her of mother. I was grim like mother, too. A paternal transference then emerged; I would abandon her and not protect her. Just prior to our summer vacation, six months into our work, a positive paternal transference began to emerge. Although potentially violent, father was not phony or pretentious like mother.

Our working alliance strengthened as we worked on her anxiety in dealing with her own patients. Conflicts about her femininity and masculine identification entered the analysis. She felt she would "lose" something in a relationship with a man. There was a beginning recognition of projection of her own castrating wishes onto men. The transference changed into predominantly a negative maternal one. She thought I was disdainful of her and directed much anger at me. She worried I would feel burdened by the lability of her moods. It was helpful to get her to appreciate that by focusing on how she processed external reality I was not denying the relevancy of it for her. She became more accepting of her externalization and more allied with me. After one year she realized how easily she felt provoked, and how "over-the- top" her anger was. She recognized she feared a lack of crises.

There was an enhancement of her feminity and she expressed gratitude for her analysis. She now recognized that feeling anxious did not mean going crazy. She began to see me as a good father figure but expressed no curiosity about me. I wondered if this was so because she felt excluded from my life. After I brought her attention to a parapraxis having to do with sexual gender, she threatened to quit, to make me "skittish." Countertransference emerged and I dismissed her ten minutes early one session. She experienced my behavior as due to a seduction on her part reminiscent of sex play with her brother. Insofar as I was able to openly discuss our enactment, I was experienced as more "real" and she became more accepting of sexual resistance. She was defending against shame and guilt in feeling responsible for both brother's and father's emotional issues because of her sexuality, e.g., sitting on her father's lap. Sitting in my waiting room was like sitting on father's lap. I began to point out when she got angry I temporarily lost her as a patient. I learned mother insinuated she was crazy and this evoked murderous rage that was then projected.

There was a linking up of her enemas, surgery and castration beliefs. She externalized the belief that her body was her enemy and the external world seemed malevolent. Mother was held responsible for father's fate; she worried she was like her mother, a sadist. She would avenge her father and absolve her guilt by destroying her mother/analyst. She suppressed loving feelings towards me because she worried I would misconstrue them as erotic. She had a dream where she was the mistress of the President and I could interpret the positive Oedipal implications. Soon thereafter for the first time triangular Oedipal material came to the fore. A female supervisor, linked to me, served as a bad mother, a displacement from my wife. When she missed sessions because of illness, she forced herself to come in because she wanted to tell me she really missed me.

She agreed with my interpretation that she was acting out erotic feelings towards me by becoming attracted to a male supervisor, a friend of mine. She talked about leaving town once she obtained her degree. A dream pointed to maternal aspects of her relationship with father that she was attracted to. I became the mother/witch analyst that would kill her. She knew it was irrational, but missed sessions without cancelling. She would imagine my suffering. It was her sadism that made her anxious. Paranoid-like terror followed after projecting her sadism onto the external world.

After obtaining her degree she accepted a job in another city. She asked to sit up in our last week. She had been in analysis for nearly four years. While attending a conference in another city she fell in love with a married man. She realized she was acting out a fantasy that was linked with her ending with me, and one where she could be very disappointed because of his marital status. She became more realistic about the limits of her new relationship, and recognized an attitudinal change about further analysis. She wondered if she could write after feeling more settled. I never received any correspondence.

Case #5)

The analysand, a Caucasian male, was in his mid-twenties working as an occupational therapist for the past five years. He was experiencing life long envy of his younger sister. His therapist, who was leaving town, referred him to me for a low fee analysis. He was overweight, with a boyish appearance. He had been living with a woman for a number of years, with an intention of someday marrying. His grandmother was a major caregiver when he and his sib were separated from his parents because of father's hospitalization for an illness. Both parent were in health professions.

The initial transference was a displacement of unresolved feelings and thoughts from his previous female therapist. He expected me to be sarcastic, impatient, scrutinizing, and humiliating. By the fourth month a paternal transference seemed to be developing. Father had an avocational interest in psychiatry. We discovered a hidden agenda was to try to confuse me as he did father and thereby feel power over me. With this understanding there was a reduction in resistance, less externalization of his Superego, so he became more accepting that his conflict was internalized. A countertransference issue during this early part of his analysis was my impatience in reaction to his attempts to "stump-the-expert" via tedious repetitiveness and passivity. I interpreted how he seemed to experience my "rules" such as charging for missed appointments, as similar to father's prohibiting his masturbation. This allowed him to bring competitive feelings into the paternal transference. Anxiety and guilt appeared about not conforming to the ideal patient/child that he felt his analyst/parents wanted. He forgot to attend a panel for nurses, an acting out of a fear that in my absence he would take the analyst/father's place with the nurse/mother, as he felt he had done as a five-year-old boy when father was out of the home convalescing.

After I returned from a vacation, he took one. He was doing to the analyst/parent what was done to him, namely "abandonment" (22 months and 5 years of age) when mother left to be with his convalescing father. I interpreted his "reversal of roles," wanting me to feel helpless, rejected, and angry while he was feeling like a powerful, self-indulging adult/parent. I represented the voice of reason and prohibition. After fifteen months of analysis he fantasized mother as a sexually aggressive woman who shot (castrated) her husband in the chest. More tender feelings for father emerged. He began to play a competitive sport, the first time in six years around this time.

When he saw me downtown he did not look at whom I was with because if it was my wife he might find her attractive and he would feel like a competitor. The solution to all this was to be loved by the father/analyst in a way that father loved his sister, namely, a helpless, dependent girl. He tried to exasperate me with pleas to be taken care of. He was amazed that he was feeling all this at a time he was also feeling outside of analysis more autonomous and independent, which suggested a transference neurosis was established. He felt he had to remain overweight so as to not overpower father. He saw me downtown again, but this time he felt a kinship insofar as we lived in the same world, but he also became aware of how little he knew me. Instead of destroying me to obtain my status, he wanted it conferred on him. A passive-feminine position was safer. He became discontented with his willingness to be castrated. His use of identification with me as defense against destructive impulses was interpreted. It was his sexual greed regarding his mother that he felt threatened his father. He felt me to be adult and himself to be a child. There was masochistic pleasure when he felt he was not being cared for. Hidden in each experience of defeat was a victory.

After our second summer vacation, he grew a mustache. He was more accepting of his masculinity. He recalled as a five year old having sexual play with a girl who later married father's friend. It felt as if father stole his girlfriend. I reconstructed positive Oedipal fantasies. For the first time he expressed anger at me for not "making him better." He felt humiliated doing "woman's work" as an occupational therapist. This belief was a defense against competitiveness and destructiveness against father.

Sex was an undercurrent in the analysis. He wanted me to "prod." He used to worry about being homosexual. Childhood fears of castration came to the surface. He no longer felt intimidated by his girlfriend and he proposed marriage, which she accepted. He the made an admission of his most carefully guarded secret, namely, that since the age of thirteen he had been cutting out magazine pictures of women with guns or drawing such women, which he then used to masturbate. This material entered the transference. He had a fantasy of discovering me shot by the previous patient, a female with a gun. There was an unconscious part where the woman with the gun has come from killing his father. He succeeds then in convincing the woman not to hurt him.

As a boy he identified with his male pony that showed dominance over his sister's pony by eating its food; the parallel was that the analysand overate too. He assumed the missionary position during sexual intercourse with his wife. However, he ejaculated prematurely. Talking about this to me made him feel humiliated as he felt as a boy seeing father's bigger penis. He felt himself to be an assassin. He had a fantasy of pushing me off the road with his car and my car ends up in a ditch. If I got angry the next session he'd punch me in the face. As a child he vowed not to live up to his potential as a way to "get even" with his parents. He'd do the same with me by being a failed analysand.

Following this there was a major shift in the transference. He felt the wish to displace father in status and the wish to be taken care of had come together; he wanted neither and felt nearly ready to terminate the analysis. He recalled as a child he was frightened that father could not set limits, and that mother was stronger than father. He soon thereafter accidentally cut his finger. Within the paternal transference I could convincingly point out the passive-into-active defense. What followed was understanding that the gun in his masturbation fantasy was a "penis." I interpreted his construction of an image of his mother as a "phallic" woman. This was impactful. He said the only thing he needed to fear was self-castration.

We set a termination in three months time. Material about his beloved and feared grandmother emerged. The little boy part of him felt abandoned by the ending of our work and pre-Oedipal issues emerged. In the transference the battle was his stubborn refusal to grow up, whereas earlier as a child it was around toilet mastery. He began to see my flaws that made me less than a perfect analyst. Psychoanalysis, he came to believe, was no guarantee to happiness without conflicts, a myth he had held to. He and his wife decided to become parents. He felt different; now he wanted to become an adult. As we approached ending he felt sad but felt strong and recognized that work remained to be done, e.g., losing weight and career planning, but felt confident he could do it independently.

His devoted grandmother was present for both separation from his parents, one at a pre-Oedipal age and the other when he was in the Oedipal stage. This facilitated the prior separation and its consequences to be organized into his dominant phase, the Oedipal Complex, and this made the pre-Oedipal conflict much more amenable to resolution. This plus his high intelligence, and psychological mindedness, once his resistances were reduced, were assets in our work. Once he became aware of the costs to him of being neurotic he was very motivated to grow up. I think these factors account for the short duration, three ½ years, of his successful analysis.

When I trained as a child and adolescent analyst, we had not yet revised our thinking to recognize that parents needed to be seen regularly to work on their parenting, to forge a working alliance with the child/adolescent analyst, etc. So I do not have process notes of parent work from this era. Because of this and reasons of anonymity and confidentiality of my more contemporary parent work done conjointly with analysis of their children, I regret I cannot illustrate such work. I do, however, want to give a vignette of work in "parent guidance" with a mother of a two year old, and a "follow-up" meeting with the parents of a latency boy I saw whose parents were seen by a social work colleague in a day treatment setting.

Case #6)

A mother of a two year old having outbursts of anger that made mother anxious was seen a total of twelve times. I explained there were different causes for temper tantrums and this helped her to realize her son was anxious. She recognized she became angry when interrupted by her son. Next she recognized she was fearful of the intensity of her own feelings so she could not help her son with his anxiety when he experienced her anger. We explored the origin of her fear of the intensity of her feelings. She delayed my meeting her son until she delved deeper into her own feelings. Soon we understood the intergenerational transmission of psychopathology across three generations. We saw how her son's anal phase with all the associated aggressive derivatives made her anxious because of experiences during her own childhood anal phase.

Case #7)

I saw the parents of an adopted latency age boy I had seen for just over three years, a month after I had ended with their son. They wondered if they needed to lower their expectations of their son who was not living up to them. They described his behavior in an extreme way, but my impression was that it was not extraordinary. Basically they seemed worried he would not be capable of becoming an independent adult. Privately, I wondered if their own anxiety about ending work with the social worker they saw regularly was exacerbating their worries about their son.

I pointed out that they temperamentally were reflective while their son was more action oriented. I indicated when their son is interested in an activity he exercises more control. He shows lack of control especially at Sunday School. Father related an incident where his son misbehaved at a religious education program organized by father that caused father to cry. His son apologized and made great effort to have his parents proud of him. Father used this example to illustrate his disappointment in his son. I emphasized how the incident was significant, as it seemed to be their son's genuine attempt to inculcate their values, show empathy, and wish to please them. Mother wondered if he would have done this if her husband had not showed his feelings so openly. I said that what her husband did was positive and perhaps more open expression of feelings with their son would allow the nature of their relationship and the bond between them to be more genuine.

I also raised the issue of adoption. They always denied this as a problem area for their son. I said he struggles with it, perhaps silently, and his rebellion may be reflected in his conflicts about accepting their values and life style. In adolescence there may be intensification about this issue. I told them he had an average IQ and that his educational goals would have to keep this in mind. At the end they spoke of the many positive changes they have seen over the time he was in day treatment and analysis. They recognized the areas of interest that do enhance his self esteem, e.g., athletics and musical instrument training. I encourage them to share our meeting with their son.

Part Four

Other Schools of Psychoanalysis

I will mention four other schools of psychoanalysis. My comments will be very brief and succinct. My aim is to bring their existence to the reader's attention. If what is said interests you then you can follow it up with more reading. The reader should keep in mind that I am not in any way an expert about these orientations. I have not practiced them and nor have I immersed myself in the scholarship written about their theory and technique. It is possible that a practitioner of one of these schools will criticize my focus as incorrect. Nevertheless, I will give my impression of the shortcomings of these schools based on my attendance at presentations and discussions. Despite this, I believe these schools have made valuable contributions. I believe that contemporary ego psychology, the more classical theory and technique I have written about above, has integrated some of the theory and technique of these methods. It is also my belief that several of these schools have in their efforts to revise the classical school have, so to speak, "thrown out the baby with the bathwater." Particularly, several have de-emphasized the significance of the instinctual drives, which, in my opinion, is a mistake.

First, I mention the Kleinian school of psychoanalysis. Here there is an emphasis on the significance of the preoedipal years of children. I think the theory demands more cognitive maturity to account for the dynamics of the period than I think exist in very young children. Nevertheless, it has brought more attention to these early years of development and has raised the awareness of ego psychologists that while the Oedipal Complex is very important it is not the only significant period of development in early childhood. The Kleinian focus on *projective identification*, a concept that postulates that an analysand projects or attributes something of themselves, e.g., a conflicted wish, onto the analyst who identifies with it and believes the origin of the wish to be within his or her own psyche, in my opinion, laid the foundation for interest in countertransference. I believe this is so because projective identification focused on the effects of analysands on their analysts to cause behavior imposed on the analytic material by analysts.

Secondly, mention should be made to the Self psychologists. They focused on the importance of deficiencies or deficits involving narcissism in personality development. This school has elucidated the varied kinds of transference that seriously disturbed narcissistic personalities evidence in the analytic situation. They seek an omnipotent object that they can merge with to heal the damaged Self. This is called a *selfobject*. Self-psychologists underscore the importance of *empathy* as a strategy. Ego psychologists have become more aware of these various transferences and hence are more sensitive to narcissistic issues in their analysands. Empathy is valued but not as a technical strategy; it more a way of relating with compassion to people who seek our help. Interpretation is, rather, our main technical strategy.

Thirdly, there is the relational school of psychoanalysis. Here the relationship between the analyst and analysand is held to be the venue or site where a "psychoanalytic cure" takes place. I agree that psychoanalysis is a procedure involving two people, not only a patient and an authoritative analyst. While I think there is much merit in thinking of psychoanalysis as involving two people, I feel that this focus has minimized the value of emotional understanding of instinctual drives and conflict involving them and the effects on the individual. Conflict experienced about the expression of wishes in the relationship seems to be lost and focus is on the analyst's interaction with the analysand. Focus on anxiety and guilt because of conflict is not a focus.

Finally, I bring attention to the inter-subjective school of psychoanalysis. Here the idea is that both analysand and analyst together create the subjective *analytic field*. The analyst is a participant-observer and he or she influences the analysand and vice-versa. It is as if there is no distinction between the analyst and the analysand. Each affects the other. The analyst's vulnerabilities enter the subjective field and impact on the analysand, and vice versa. My observation is that there is too much self-disclosure by the analyst. I think that this is burdensome to analysands, except in some instances. In my observation it is difficult sometimes to discern who is the analyst and who is the analysand. I mentioned earlier, focusing on enactments as a contribution of the inter-subjective school of psychoanalysis. This is a valuable contribution. In enactments the analyst's countertransference enters into the analytic field. The analyst is unaware of this happening and often it is the analysand who brings it to the analyst's attention. My opinion is that the analyst is wise to acknowledge its presence, assuming it's a valid observation, but not to do self-analysis and self-disclosure at the scene. After understanding what happened the analyst may elect to say something that is not too burdensome to account for the enactment. For example, "I think that when you were talking of your mother's death when you were young it reminded me of a grief reaction of my own that was painful. Your eventual observation was correct that we got off the topic of your grief about your mother's death. I think that's why I changed the subject." Most analysands respect this limitation of self-disclosure and appreciate knowing that the analyst is human too.

Part Five

The widening spectrum of Psychoanalytic treatment

Work with psychotics of any age, in my opinion, is treatment that is psychoanalytically informed. Again, my self-admission is that I have no experience treating this diagnostic type of patient. Colleagues who work with psychotics might claim it is a travesty to exclude such work as psychotherapy, albeit psychoanalytically informed, and not as psychoanalysis proper. There are analysts who report some remarkable positive effects. Because of delusionary thinking, hallucinations, paranoid beliefs, and defective reality testing, it would seem to me that a period of psychotherapy would be required before a more interpretive approach would be effective. The patient would need to feel safe and this would take time. I assume every patient is different in the severity of these symptoms and the duration of a more supportive and educative psychotherapy will vary.

Work with delinquent adolescents is another diagnostic category that I lack experience with. The delinquent adolescent has had a deficiency of being educated about ethical community behavior. The delinquent's Superego and Ego Ideal are ill formed or pathologically formed because of "bad parenting." It would seem to me that the analyst/therapist must first develop a trusting relationship with the adolescent with the expectation that a period of re-education will follow. A trusting relationship I presume will be an outcome of varied strategies based on the different histories of the adolescents in treatment. A positive transference will likely take time to build up. Once achieved, identification with the analyst might occur and an ethical adult imago will be internalized and a new Superego and Ego Ideal can be structured. Perhaps then, in some cases more traditional psychoanalysis can be helpful.

Part Six

Dealing
with Illness & Death

Existential anxiety issues are always there for everyone but often do not surface until older age, or if one has a serious, sometimes potentially fatal illness. In young children, death may be a theme, but they often do not recognize the permanency of death until age eight or nine. Adolescents often do not think of it because the issues of puberty and becoming more autonomous individuals takes "center stage." But for older people who recognize that more of their lives are behind them than ahead of them, death is an issue.

Religiously observant people struggle less with dying insofar as they often embrace a concept of the soul and eternal life. But for the majority of adults dying is recognized as inevitable and some put the fact out of consciousness, while others deal with it or struggle with it.

In analysis when an analysand talks about thoughts and feelings about dying, the analyst, too, must deal with their own corresponding feelings and thoughts evoked by the analytic process. An analyst must empathically and compassionately point out that the analysand seems to have death on their mind. The analyst will convey that this is something that can be talked about, and that thinking about it is not pathological. Hopefully, the analysand will proceed to reflect on the subject. The analyst, too, will do some self-analysis about how the subject affects them.

If an analyst is due to have a planned surgery and will need to cancel some sessions, should this be disclosed to an analysand? I think that it depends upon whether it will be obvious or not, e.g., using crutches. The issue of boundaries and consideration as to whether such a disclosure will or will not violate the existing boundary is paramount here. But consideration of boundaries is relative. I think crossing a boundary is not done casually but done with forethought and carefully. Of course, if an analysand cannot attend sessions and is in hospice at home, boundaries will be put aside and a session will be conducted in the analysand's home or via Skype.

A Professional Will

It is professional, ethical, and the responsibility of every analyst to draw up a professional will. In this document there will be instructions to a colleague chosen and agreeing to execute the will, about how to identify one's patients and supervisees and their telephone numbers, to inform them of your unexpected death. Further instructions might be where folders on patients are kept, putting an announcement on your phone that the practice is closed, how to identify the balance of outstanding fees owed by patients and analysands, etc. Additional instructions will be given about the destruction of files. The executor of your professional will now will decide with the patients as to whether or not they would like a referral to talk about the unexpected ending of their treatment, your death, and their grief, etc.

Planned Retirement by the Analyst

Analysand's, I think, best be given sufficient time to plan and react to their analyst's planned retirement. What is sufficient time? I think one year suffices as a reasonable amount of time. An analysand's reactions when told will be immediate and then recede and then resurface, as the date of the forced ending is close. Some analysands will regret learning about the retirement; others may be pleased but suppress saying this. In either case, learning about one's analyst's retirement likely will trigger memories of other "endings." What I have in mind are endings such as going off to college in another city or state, leaving the parental home, moving out of state where you spent your childhood for a job, etc. Then there are also grief reactions to endings such as a grandparent's death, the divorce of parents, etc. Hopefully, during the ensuing year these thoughts and feelings can be analyzed and worked through. Some analysands may elect to end the analysis before the planned ending, thereby turning *passive-into-active*, a defense, to leave rather than be left. With each analysand consideration as to whether or not a suggestion of continued work with a colleague should be made. Some analysands will raise this possibility. If this possibility seems feasible, a referral can be made. I think it best be made before ending so the analysand can have a consultation prior to ending and have the possibility of talking about their reactions to their analyst.

As one ages, one may develop cognitive impairments and this eventuality can also affect analysts. Hopefully, the analyst does not utilize denial and he or she notices the diminished effectiveness on being an analyst. One's analysands often do not bring this to the attention of the analyst. A planned retirement is the sensible option.

Negative Therapeutic Reaction

Rarely in an analysis that is going well, where the process seems to be deepening, suddenly an interpretation is made and there is a worsening of the analysand's condition. It can be bewildering to the analyst. It would seem that "things were going too well." The analysand maybe feels guilty that he or she is undeserving of feeling better, experiencing less guilt and anxiety. It is akin to "survivior guilt." It may be that there is an underlying masochistic streak that went unnoticed up to this point. With more analytic work and insight on the analysand's part, hopefully, the treatment can renew a progressive trajectory.

"Soul Murder"

There are some patients that have been so traumatized by an abusive past, perhaps by a disturbed parent, that it would seem that their very essence has been damaged, their "soul." There is no joy in their lives. These patients dissociate from the Self that has been "destroyed." They lose their identity. Like with some children who need ego strengthening psychotherapy before child analysis is embarked upon, such adult patients will need to build up a sense of trust in psychotherapy before they will risk "getting in touch" with their Self and exposing it to another. It makes sense to me that the analyst be consistent and that a change of professional not take place.

Diversity

Psychoanalysis has not had a long history of treating people of color, so having the analyst and analysand be of different races is a relatively new experience. Psychoanalytic Institutes in the United State only in the past two decades have been training non-Caucasian candidates. As a result, analysts are becoming more sensitive to the need to pay attention to their analysands' feelings about racial differences between the two of them. Also, countertransference sensitivities need to be attended to. Analysands may be reluctant to speak openly about their perceptions and feelings, being apprehensive that they may be seen as accusing the analyst as being racist, or by their disclosures revealing their own racist predilections. Analysts can intervene, by pointing out that everyone has some racism as part of their psychology, zenophobia, that regrettably is inculcated by one's social culture, a form of vestigial tribalism.

Part Seven

Postscript

Why did I decide to write this book? I am sure that there are multiple motives for writing this book. The one that I would like to speak to is the following. Psychoanalysis will never be popular. This is because it deals with a subject that most people would prefer not to think about, and certainly not talk about. The idea that civilized human beings unconsciously have base instincts like other animals is an abhorrent idea to many people. That Freud focused on the sexual and aggressive instincts made matters even worse for civilized and religious people. They did not consider that Freud was not advocating the free expression of basic unconscious drives. He was all for self-control and sublimation of aims.

In popular Western culture when psychoanalysts are portrayed in movies or in drama, often they are fools or corrupt. It used to be that they were shown to be silent and busy taking notes. But this misrepresentation or caricature of analysts, I think is a way of demeaning the goals of psychoanalysis, self-actualization, understanding the past so it does not repeat itself in the present, learning to forgive oneself for transgressions so you can forgive others, etc. It also gets back to an uneasiness that another can know more about you then you know about yourself. I am hesitant to disclose that I am a psychoanalyst when invariably asked at a social gathering, "So what kind of work do you do?" Some people openly say, "Oh, I better watch myself." I let them know that, "I'm off for the day."

Anna Freud is seldom mentioned any more in child studies about development or pathology. Why is it that her valuable contribution is neglected? Also, new schools of psychoanalysis have started originally to revise the field but they seem in some respects to be trying to replace the "classical school." They have valuable contribution to make but what was indispensible in the classical school seems to become dispensable.

The "zeitgeist" in contemporary psychiatry is a biological orientation. Indeed, the mind and the brain are connected and someday in the future we will know how. But, in my opinion, this is not in the near future. And even so, if by "tweaking" the brain we could change the mind I would still want to know why the mind worked in the way it did before the biological intervention. "A life not understood is not a life worth living."

Medication is the treatment of choice in most Psychiatry departments in the States. Residents are not taught to listen to their patients but instead have a questionnaire to be asked in order to arrive at a diagnosis so that a drug can be prescribed. Very young children are given diagnoses requiring medication that often have dire side effects. Diagnoses in child psychiatry become popular and are over-used. Kids who are anxious are diagnosed as hyperactive with attention deficit disorder. Instead of drugs the more appropriate disposition would be psychotherapy for them and their parents. But when you are dealing with almost thirty children in a classroom, a teacher wants quick results and medication to "numb" such a child is sought.

Patients want quick results. Understandably, when you have symptoms that burden you, impatience is to be expected. But symptom removal is not sufficient. Patients need to be educated that a symptom is a neurotic "solution" to a "mental conflict." The conflict needs to be processed lest the symptom reappears or another different one will appear. Insurance companies, too, want quick results so that the period of paying out benefits is shortened. One consequence of this has been the development of treatments such as "Cognitive Behavior Therapy." The claim is that the goal should be symptom removal not resolution of conflict. Under the mantel of being "evidence based treatment" CBT has become popular. Statistics can be used to point out that the symptom has gone and has not been replaced. Psychoanalysis is said not to be evidence based. But the results of a treatment such as analysis cannot be assessed by a simple questionnaire. Also, there is statistical evidence to show the effectiveness of psychoanalysis as a treatment. Besides, there are many "testimonials" from former analysands attesting to the value of their analysis. Skeptics will say that after a lot of cost and time, what else would you expect a former analysand to say. I am pleased to say that I have heard sincere testimonials from former adult patients and parents of children and adolescents I have seen.

The above accounts for why I wrote this book. I hope to make more understandable a process that is private and misrepresented. I hope, too, that more people will consider consultations for themselves and their children to learn if an analysis is the "treatment of choice." For this to happen on a larger scale, psychoanalysts need to reduce their fees whenever possible. I know one needs to "make a living" but if money is the reason for choosing to be an analyst then going into a "helping profession" is probably the wrong choice. Psychoanalytic Institutes need to establish clinics staffed by candidate analysts and supervised by graduate analysts. Reduced fee treatment can be an option as well as insurance covered treatment.

Representative
List of Topics

Preface   p.1
Psychoanalytic Concepts of Development   p.5
    Psychosexual Phases,
    Characteristics of Drives,
    Fixation & Regression
    Complemental Series
    Adolescent Development
    Adult Development
Psychoanalytic Model of the Mind   p.9
    Ucs., Pcs. Cs.
    Topographic Model
    Structural Model
    Characteristics of Id, Superego, & Ego
    Ego Ideal/ Ideal Self
    Ego Functions
    Self, Identity & Identifications
    Mental Conflict
Referral   p.15
    Initial contact with Adult
    Seeing Parents First with Young Children
    Initial Contact with Adolescent
Evaluation   p.17
    Analyzability
    Trial Analysis?
    "Rule" of Abstinence
    Reparative Therapy First

Initial Face to Face Contact
The "Fit" between analytic couple
Recommendation   p.21
Procedures with Different Age Groups
Common Questions Asked
The Frame   p.23
Issues of Confidentiality
Immersion
Cancellations
Office Setups
Note Taking
The Beginning of an Analysis   p.27
Use of Couch
Free Association
Feeling Safe
Establishing a Working Alliance   p.31
Self Observation & Self Experiencing
Helping Inner Child in Adult to Grow Up
Alliance with Parents of Adolescents and Children
Distinction Between Thoughts & Deeds
Lessening of Guilt
Resistance   p.34
Ubiquity of Resistance
Examples of Resistance
Signal anxiety
Ego defenses
Absence of Dreams
Secrets
Topic of Masturbation with Adolescents
Avoidance of Curiosity About Analyst
Young Children and Resistance
Sexual Gender Issues and Resistance
Use of Defenses in Resistance
Character Defense

Transference   p.40
   Positive and Negative
   Transference Cure
   Transference with young Children
   Timing of Interpretation
   Transference with Adolescents
   Erotic Transference
   Transference Neurosis
Real Object, Developmental Object, Transference Object   p.44
   Definition
Countertransference   p.46
   Manifestations
   Enactments
   Free Floating Attention
   Love in the dyadic relationship
Interpretation   p.49
   Definition & purpose
   Interpretations as Conjectures
   Surface to Depth
   Adolescents and Interpretation
      Struggles with masturbation
   Reconstruction
   Trauma
   Adolescence and Separation
   Masturbation
   Clarification & Confrontation
   Interpretations as Conjectures
Acting Out   p.58
   Definition
   Acting out and Resistance
Limit Setting   p.60
   Violation of the Frame
   Answering Questions
   Boundaries

Children and Limits
Requests for medications
Ways of Bringing Material   p.66
 Deciding on an Agenda
 Traumatic Memories
 Telephone sessions
 Dreams
 Bringing a Pet
 Play
 Toys
 Playful thought with Adolescents
 Music
Comings and Goings   p.73
 Punctuality/Lateness
 Departures
Role of Education   p.75
 Neutrality
  Departures
 Normalizing some feelings
  Depression
  Guilt
 Confronting an Abuser
Work with Parents   p.78
 Value in Work with Children & Adolescents
 Difficulties
 Defining a child's "problems"
 Issues of Confidentiality
 Parents and Infants
Goals of Psychoanalytic Treatment   p.82
 Analysand's Goals
 Analyst's Goals
Working Through   p.85
 Repetition
 Overcoming Resistance
 Repetition Compulsion

Eradication of Conflict
Progressive Movement
Termination   p.87
Analysis of Major Conflicts
Quality of Transference
Issues
Sadness/Grief
Follow Up
Earlier Leave-taking Experiences

Part Three
Brief Clinical Illustrations   p.93

Part Four
Other Schools of Psychoanalysis   p.111
Revision of Classical School
Kleinian
Self psychology
Relational
Inter-Subjective

Part Five
Widening Spectrum of psychoanalytic Treatment p.117
Work with Psychotics
Work with Delinquent Adolescents

Part Six
Dealing with Illness & Death   p.121
Existential Anxiety
A Professional Will   p.123
Definition
Planned Retirement of Analyst   p.124
Telling the Analysand
Cognitive Impairment of Analyst
Negative Therapeutic Reaction   p.125
Definition

Soul Murder   p.126
    Definition
Diversity   p.127
    Racism as ubiquitous

Part Seven
Postscript   p.131
    Reasons for writing the book

Representative List of Topics   p.135

Recommended Readings   p.141

Recommended Readings

Child Analysis

The Psychoanalytic Study of the Child, Vol 1-67, International Universities Press, NY 1945-70

Quadrangle, NY 1971-72

Yale University Press, CT 1973-2015

Routledge, Phila, PA 2016-

Bulletin of the Hampstead Clinic, Vol 1-7, 1978-83

Bulletin of the Anna Freud Centre, Vol 8-18, 1984-1995

Child Analysis, Vol 1-18

Child Analysis & Therapy, John Glenn (ED.), Jason Aronson, NY, 1978

The Psychoanalytic Works of Hansi Kennedy, Jill M. Miller & Carla Neely (Eds.) Karnac: London, 2008

The Many Meanings of Play, Albert J. Solnit, Donald J.Cohen, Peter B. Neubauer, Yale University Press, New Haven & London, 1993

Studies in Child Psychoanalysis: Pure and Applied. Monograph Series PSC, #5, Yale Universities Press, New Haven & London, 1975

The Technique of Child Psychoanalysis: Discussions With Anna Freud, Joseph Sandler, Hansi Kennedy, Robert L. Tyson (Eds) Harvard University Press, Cambridge, MA, 1980

Rosenbaum, A.L. The assessment of parental functioning: A critical process in the evaluation of children for Psychoanalysis. *Psa Q.,* 1994, 63: 466-90

Working With Parents Makes Therapy Work, Kerry Kelly Novick & Jack Novick, Jason Aronson, NY, 2005

Adolescent Psychoanalysis

The Psychoanalytic Study of the Child, Vol 1-70

The Analyst & the Adolescent at Work, Marjorie Harley (Ed), Quadrangle, NY, 1974

Developmental Breakdown and Psychoanalytic Treatment in Adolescense, Moses Laufer & M. Egle Laufer (Eds), Yale University Press, New Haven & London, 1989

The Suicidal Adolescent Moses Laufer (Ed) International Universities Press, CT., 1995

Adult Psychoanalysis

Freud's Rules of Deream Interprtetation, Alexander Grinstein, International Universitites Press, CT., 1983

On Beginning an Analysis, Theodore J. Jacobs & Arnold Rothstein (Eds), International Universities Press, CT, 1990

Psychoanalytic Technique and the Creation of Analytic Patients, Arnold Rothstein, International Universities Press, CT., 1995

The Interpretation of Dreams in Clinical Work, Workshop Series, American Psychoanalytical Association, Monograph 3, Arnold Rothstein (Ed), International Universities Press, CT., 1987

The Technique & Practice of Psychoanalysis 1, Ralph R. Greenson, International Universities Press, NY, 1967

The Technique & Practice of Psychoanalysis 2, Alan Sugarman, Robert A. Nemiroff, Daniel P. Greenson, (Eds), International Universities Press, CT., 1992

The Patient & the Analyst, Joseph Sandler, Christopher Dare, Alex Holder (Eds), International Universities Press, NY, 1973

www.ingramcontent.com/pod-product-compliance
Lightning Source LLC
Chambersburg PA
CBHW050730030426
42336CB00012B/1502